ACCESSING AWARENESS AND DEVELOPING KNOWLEDGE

Foundations for Skill in a Multicultural Society

EDITION

3

ACCESSING AWARENESS AND DEVELOPING KNOWLEDGE

Foundations for Skill in a Multicultural Society

PATRICK MCGRATH
National-Louis University

JOHN A. AXELSON
Emeritus Northern Illinois University

Brooks/Cole Publishing Company

I(T)P® An International Thomson Publishing Company

Pacific Grove • Albany • Belmont • Bonn • Boston • Cincinnati • Detroit • Johannesburg • London
Madrid • Melbourne • Mexico City • New York • Paris • Singapore • Tokyo • Toronto • Washington

Sponsoring Editor: *Eileen Murphy*
Marketing Team: *Steve Catalano, Aaron Eden, and Jean Thompson*
Editorial Assistant: *Susan C. Carlson*
Production Coordinator: *Mary Vezilich*

Production Service: *Scratchgravel Publishing Services*
Manuscript Editor: *Betty Berenson*
Cover and Illustration: *Sharon Kinghan*
Typesetting: *Scratchgravel Publishing Services*
Printing and Binding: *Patterson Printing*

For more information, contact:

BROOKS/COLE PUBLISHING COMPANY
511 Forest Lodge Road
Pacific Grove, CA 93950
USA

International Thomson Publishing Europe
Berkshire House 168-173
High Holborn
London WC1V 7AA
England

Thomas Nelson Australia
102 Dodds Street
South Melbourne, 3205
Victoria, Australia

Nelson Canada
1120 Birchmount Road
Scarborough, Ontario
Canada M1K 5G4

International Thomson Editores
Seneca 53
Col. Polanco
115060 México, D. F., México

International Thomson Publishing GmbH
Königswinterer Strasse 418
53227 Bonn
Germany

International Thomson Publishing Asia
60 Albert Street
#15-01 Albert Complex
Singapore 189969

International Thomson Publishing Japan
Hirakawacho Kyowa Building, 3F
2-2-1 Hirakawacho
Chiyoda-ku, Tokyo 102
Japan

Printed in the United States of America

10 9 8 7 6 5 4 3 2 1

Library of Congress Cataloging-in-Publication Data

McGrath, Patrick, [date]–
    Accessing awareness and developing knowledge : foundations for skill in a multicultural society / Patrick McGrath, John A. Axelson.
    — 3rd ed.
        p.   cm.
    ISBN 0-534-34495-X (alk. paper)
    1. Cross-cultural counseling—United States—Problems, exercises, etc.   2. Minorities—Counseling of—United States—Problems, exercises, etc.   3. Counseling—United States—Problems, exercises, etc.   4. Multiculturalism—United States—Problems, exercises, etc. 5. Pluralism (Social sciences)—United States—Problems, exercises, etc.   I. Axelson, John A., [date]– . II. Title.
BF637.C6M3789   1999
305'.076—dc21
                                                    98-16305
                                                       CIP

CONTENTS

SECTION III
Heightening Our Awareness and Knowledge of Others   59

SECTION IV
Awareness and Knowledge of Sociopolitical Issues   82

SECTION V
Getting Ahead in the United States   99

SECTION VI
Growth and Development   124

SECTION VII
Approaches to Counseling and Counseling Interactions   163

SECTION VIII
Multiculturalism as a Force and Influence
in Human Relationships   195

ACKNOWLEDGMENTS

In this edition we have updated social and economic data and provided important points for your consideration at the beginning of each section. Although many of the exercises and activities are rather timeless—that is, they are as appropriate now as they were in years past and will be in the future—we have added a number of new activities as well.

We wish to thank our students at National-Louis University and Northern Illinois University who have used the material in this manual and offered helpful comments and suggestions. Appreciation is also extended to our many colleagues who encouraged us to pursue the work involved in creating an experiential manual for multicultural counseling and development. We would certainly be remiss if we did not also thank our many colleagues in the American Counseling Association, the American Psychological Association, and the National Association of Social Workers who have been so kind and helpful in their responses to the first edition of this manual. We are especially appreciative of the assistance given by Professors George Litman and Bob Green of National-Louis University. Professor Green has since died, but his contributions continue to inspire us. The resources in Appendix A, which are used in Activity III-8, Cultural Profiles, and in Activity III-9, Activities to Discover Human Diversity, were developed in conjunction with him. Professor Green instructed courses in the psychology of culture and self, the psychology of development, and theories of personality. In addition, we extend our gratitude to Dr. Roger Herring of the University of Arkansas at Little Rock for his invaluable assistance.

The production and readability of this manual have been enhanced by the expert talents and processing skills of the Integrated Curriculum Services at National-Louis University. We also wish to acknowledge the support for the project that was provided by the administration of National-Louis University and, in particular, Dr. Edward Risinger, Dean of the College of Arts and Sciences.

We thank the staff at Brooks/Cole Publishing Company for the excellent cooperation and help they provided us. We are very much appreciative of the gentle but persistent prodding to stay on target, first from Claire Verduin and continuing from Eileen Murphy. Their encouragement, support, and directions have guided us in completing this edition. We also thank those who took their time and energy to review our work: Roberto Cortez Gonzalez, The University of Texas at El Paso; Linda Roddy, Northern Arizona University; and Russell E. Thomas, University of Memphis.

Finally, we acknowledge that one's cultural awareness and understanding are interwoven with one's family experiences. We especially appreciate the support, encouragement, and teachings shared by our families. Many thanks to the transcultural McGrath family—Denise Hertz, Zachary Choe, and Justin Teague. Many thanks also to the extended Axelson family—Ernestine Delventhal; Kristin, Tom, and Lola; and Jon, Cindy, and their children, Erik and Lynea.

Patrick McGrath
John A. Axelson

Introduction

Accessing Awareness and Developing Knowledge: Foundations for Skill in a Multicultural Society is designed to assist, encourage, and challenge readers to more fully develop their awareness and knowledge of self and others in a pluralistic society. This manual presents experiential and cognitive activities and exercises to help learners access and develop a multicultural sensitivity to and knowledge of persons of different cultural beliefs, values, and behaviors. Although developed to accompany *Counseling and Development in a Multicultural Society* (3rd ed.), this manual, we believe, will also be of value when used in conjunction with other texts of cross-cultural content. One foci of our learners' manual is directed to the preparation of human services/counseling practitioners. However, as we approach the 21st century, it should also be useful to a wide array of people and professions concerned with relating to diverse populations and issues within the United States as well as relating to people of other countries.

We hope that our work will assist you in accessing and developing:

1. Your appreciation of the influences of one's cultural heritage upon the self.

2. Your understanding and valuing of the cultural values, beliefs, and behaviors of persons of a different heritage.

3. Your sensitivity to and knowledge of the diversity and complexity of the relationship between people of differing backgrounds and experience in general and specifically in counseling and human services work.

4. Your ability to enjoy your own and others' cultural similarities and differentnesses.

5. Your recognition of the influences and interactional relationships your own and others' heritage and self-identity have with your membership in national and global societies.

Learning Multiculturalism

Human learning is embedded in social processes—that is, in processes of gaining self-awareness through experiencing one's self and experiencing others. Self-awareness is encouraged by accessing information and by developing a self-trusting yet critically questioning stance toward how we perceive and evaluate events, occasions, experiences, and objects of attention in our lives. As anthropologist Gregory Bateson suggests in *Steps to an Ecology of Mind* (New York: Dutton, 1972), information is "a difference that makes a difference." Thus, in accessing information, you are taking the first step in making yourself the most important instrument in your learning.

Learning occurs by personally applying and relating ideas, information, tasks, or experiences to that which we already know. It is further suggested that cognitive understandings can be maximized in the context of examining an experience as perceived, shared, and compared by all involved in it.

We hope that the exercises, the experiences suggested, and the questions for reflection encourage you to discover meaningful aspects of yourself, of different others, and the way relationships between you and others are affected by such information.

In discovering and learning multicultural information that will be meaningful and useful to you, we suggest you remind yourself that we all:

1. Belong to a culturally diverse world in which our own cross-cultural experiences and understandings have already been influenced directly by those around us and indirectly by the media (newspapers, TV, etc.).

2. Often know only a modicum of the powerful influence that our own culture has had upon us. The mere fact of our birth into a particular group, while it may provide a sense of identity, does not provide us with full and complete awareness and understanding of the what and how of all of the behaviors, attitudes, and beliefs that we develop by being a member of this identity group.

3. Are limited in our understandings of self and others by the very fact that both direct and indirect sources of information, while quite influential, often provide only a selective and limited amount of information about our own as well as about another's culture.

4. Must discover the similarity and dissimilarity of influences operating upon each of us, our families, our communities, and our society in order to best understand the influences of culture upon each other. The differential aspects of each person's and each culture's experience in a pluralistic society lead to a diversity of experiences and perceptions and thus a diversity of cognitive, affective, and behavioral responses to other members of the human family.

5. Must recognize the powerful influence of our own sense of self-esteem as we discover the meanings to us of other persons and events. We need to recognize that the discovery of multicultural information will disturb and discomfort us at times. Discovering what we share and do not share will not always lead to easy acceptance of or intellectual reconciliations between divergent understandings, experiences, values, and behaviors.

The multicultural personality develops in the context of understanding self, understanding others, discovering our common dreams and directions, and appreciating our differences and living life in a complex and multifaceted society. The multicultural personality works to achieve flexibility in belonging and identifying with the whole of humanity regardless of differences that may exist. It is hoped that this learners' manual encourages a commitment to understanding yourself and others as multicultural personalities.

Multiculturalism in the Context of Life and Living

There are many kinds or levels of culture and subculture that influence thought, feeling, and behavior. Cultures and subcultures may be considered models or designs for living life. Culture, per se, is powerfully influential as we choose our behaviors to address the tasks of living. Quite simply, we must relate with and respond to our environment (people, places, things, beliefs) to most effectively negotiate life's challenges. It is our interactions with other people, both similar and dissimilar to us, that reinforce and/or encourage or discourage our awareness and understanding and help us develop our skills of living in this world.

Obviously, there are universal issues of concern among the diverse array of peoples on earth, and there are also many cultural models that guide us. How we relate to self and to others of similar heritage or experience as well as to others with different heritages or experiences is to a great extent a product of several levels of cultural influences.

Life is experienced, learning occurs, personality develops, and living is processed in the context of:

1. A self-identity that develops and is specific to our most unique inter- and intra-personal experiences.

2. A culture of family as exemplified and experienced between ourselves and those who were or are our most *immediate* caretakers and nurturers.

3. A culture of sameness—that is, those who are similar in characteristics of ethnicity, language, customs, and beliefs.

4. A subculture of influence composed of those who share a particular condition, status, or interest that may be temporary or lifelong. Examples include life stage groupings, such as teenagers and senior citizens; or conditions, such as living with a disability, being poor, being wealthy, or belonging to groups of persons bound together by common interests, such as self-help, lifestyle preference, religion, profession, career, or by leisure time interests.

5. A local or regional culture that may have developed in one's community or region of residence, such as one's neighborhood; a rural, urban, or suburban society; or a regional (Midwest, Southwest, Southern) geopolitical environment.

6. A sociopolitical, society-wide culture, which often espouses a set of dominant, national norms of behavior that may be overarching and have pervasive influence upon each citizen of an entire nation or grouping of nations. Such dominant societal influences are often articulated and operationalized through prevailing forms of constitutional government, societal institutions, and philosophies addressing

societal goals. For example, we often compare and contrast Western and Eastern philosophies and orientations, which provide both thought and guidance for living, based upon differing societal structures and basic understandings, which in turn encourage certain differing behaviors of life and living.

You are encouraged to recognize the complex interactions that occur between such levels of cultural influence as you explore your specific heritage of experiences as well as the cultural heritages of others. Your commitment to investigate and develop your own awareness and knowledge of multiculturalism can be a powerful force in your own life.

Multicultural Counseling within the Human Services

Human services professionals are expected to assist clients in searching for and reaching their desired goals. This task becomes increasingly challenging when clients' experiences and expectations differ from those of helpers. In order to begin where the client is, to appreciate the client holistically, one needs to know about the influence of the client's culture. This includes being aware of dimensions of the client's experience that are related to race/ethnicity, socioeconomic status, religion, language, education, gender, generation, geographic region, physical condition or status, and community residence. All helping professionals may concern themselves further with recognizing the influences of subcultural groups that may be unique to this client's life and living. Human services/counselor professionals ought to consider carefully not only such client influences but also the influence of such information upon themselves.

A professional helping relationship ideally is a coequal relationship in which both client and counselor coparticipate, codetermine, and coauthorize what will be done in an effort that covalidates and empowers both the client and the professional helper. The primary tool that we bring to such a relationship, regardless of our education and/or theoretical orientation, is ourselves. Not only do professionals make an effort to understand others' situations but also they must be equally committed to knowing their own values and beliefs of influence—insofar as is possible. Systemically speaking, we each have come to know ourselves in large part due to contact with others, both historically and in the present. The cultural constructs we have developed over time, as obtained from family, neighborhood, societal experiences, media, and so on, do and will influence the directions and goals we encourage and support clients to move toward. Before each of us can go forward, we must know who we are. The past informs the present and it is in the present that we create the future.

The identification and the reality of determining achievable client goals are in direct proportion to our understanding of the client's world. The client's acceptance of our ideas, directives, and encouragements is clearly related to the helper's ability to demonstrate sensitivity to and valuing of the person being assisted. Sensitivity to and awareness of others is a function of how well we are each sensitized and aware of ourself. Thus, we come full circle in developing appropriate, acceptable, and realistic goals with clients—that is, to understand the client, we need to understand ourselves, including the personal qualities, attributes, and understandings that we each bring to a relationship and that greatly influence the efficacy of helping processes.

Today, theories and approaches are being developed, or adjusted, to take into account the diverse cultural backgrounds and experiences of clients. There is no one formula available for multicultural counseling and human services work, nor do we suggest that there is a single approach best suited for working with culturally different persons. Nor do we suggest that a commonality of race or ethnicity shared by the helper and the client is automatically of high value. In point of fact, the diversity among members of the same group—even when they are of the same race/ethnicity/gender/socioeconomic status—is often so great as to mitigate against such a simplistic notion. One of our hopes would be that you examine the "differences within such differences"; thus, *all* Asian persons are not alike, *all* Black persons are not alike, *all* Native American persons are not alike, *all* White persons are not alike, *all* elderly are not alike, *all* women are not alike, *all* youth are not alike, and so on.

FOR YOUR CONSIDERATION

1. The important emphasis in this manual is on you and your discovery of your own culture and experience, your identification of its influence in your life, and then, your examination of the culture and experience of different others. If you become aware of the powerful influence of your own culture upon your own beliefs, attitudes, and behaviors and recognize how difficult it may be, at times, to change or modify your life, you will be more sensitized to what you may be asking others to change in their lives.

2. The exercises, activities, and questions are intended to stimulate and guide your learning and discovering life meanings that are important and relevant to you and others. We encourage you to discover how best to live life within that context and in a positive, healthy relationship with others who may have a different context of life and living. We hope that in working with and for others you may utilize these understandings in assisting others to move toward their own goals according to their own beliefs and in their own manner. We believe, furthermore, that personal and professional efforts of such a nature will move our pluralistic society forward for the benefit of all of us.

3. Most of the exercises in this manual are introduced with an orienting paragraph in regard to a specific activity. However, we have not attempted to encourage you to arrive at a particular conclusion. Rather, we hope that you will expand your range of awareness and from this base refine your own personal and professional knowledge of the influence and interaction of cultural experience upon and between you and others.

4. You will also find that many activities are identified as group activities. Please note that these group activities can be easily modified to become an individual activity, and you may want to do so. Nevertheless, we still encourage you to seek a diversity of opinions, perceptions, and reactions from others. Shared activities provide a rich opportunity to exchange differing viewpoints and experiences as well as to discover elements that are universally common to all humans.

5. Although some exercises, given the logistics, time requirements, and/or the requirement of additional participants may not always be feasible in light of your available schedule, it will still be useful to vicariously imagine what the results might be. Forming a discussion group to explore possible findings is another way to sensitize oneself to variations in cultural experiences and relationships.

6. *Critical Thoughts Journal:* As noted, you are encouraged to share your experiences, perceptions, and understandings, as developed in accord with the activities and exercises suggested throughout this manual. Given these experiences, you may also find that you observe, perceive, and think about events in your daily activities somewhat differently than in the past—that is, you notice things you hadn't noticed before, such as the cultural themes that may appear in a popular movie, book, or newspaper story. These "noticed differently" observations may have great meaning to you and possibly others. Such perceptions may not lend themselves to being recorded according to the structure and format of this manual. To assist you in maintaining a record of such thoughts and perceptions a "Journal of Critical Thoughts in Multi-culturalism" form is provided in Appendix C of this manual. You may find it useful to record such information week to week as you develop further understanding of this material. A summarization page for those thoughts you think most important is also provided for your use.

7. Finally, you may find that the spaces or lines allocated for your answers to specific questions or requests are not sufficient for what you want to say or how you might want to respond. The reason for this is that we did not want to fill the pages with lines and spaces. Thus, we recommend that on the allocated lines or spaces you jot down only your main ideas in a few words or use key words or phrases. If you prefer to develop your ideas or express yourself more fully, you can use separate sheets of paper, identifying your statements by the activity and page number in the manual.

An Invitation to Share Information

We, the authors, want to thank our numerous colleagues—students, faculty, and friends—who over the years have shared insights, experiences, and suggestions that have inspired us. We hope you will share with us your reactions, suggestions, or ideas that would improve this manual but, more important, be useful in improving human relationships in a multicultural society and world.

To this end, please send your information and/or idea to:

Patrick McGrath, Ed.D. and John Axelson, Ph.D.
c/o Brooks/Cole Publishing Company
511 Forest Lodge Road
Pacific Grove, CA 93950-5098
USA

I

Influences in and Understanding of Cross-Cultural Experiences

Background Reading: Chapter 1, "Culture and Counseling," in John A. Axelson, *Counseling and Development in a Multicultural Society* (3rd ed.). Pacific Grove, Calif.: Brooks/Cole 1999.

FOR YOUR CONSIDERATION

If we seek an answer based on what we already know, we may be limited to do that which provided imperfect answers in the past. That is, it is likely that past understandings may not provide the answers sought and necessary for the best resolution of present concerns. In effect, while long-standing beliefs, values, and behaviors generally provide a great sense of stability to us, they may also be a source of great limitation as new and innovative answers are needed in a changing world.

In any educational endeavor we bring with us a certain background of understanding and information based upon our life experiences. We use this information, gained in the past, to make sense of our present experience and to determine some of our future actions. Given the rapid pace of living, it seems that we often are not fully aware of how the past has influenced our present ideas and behaviors. Also, we usually do not have the luxury of assessing what it is we do know or think we know about a certain topic, person, or event prior to having a significant and often unexpected contact with such a topic, person, or event. For example, when initially meeting persons of a different race, we often rapidly form impressions about them based on attitudes and beliefs that we formed from past experiences with members of that group directly or even indirectly through television, jokes, or stories. The behavior we instantaneously display based on this past experience may very well influence the process and content of the relationship in the present moment as well as in the future.

We present the following exercises, survey instruments, and questions to assist you in identifying some of your past and present ideas, your behaviors, and your experiences of relating to persons different from yourself. These are also presented with the notion of helping you define a baseline of present knowledge about yourself and others, which can be used as a measure against the information you develop in the process of completing this manual.

ACTIVITY I-1
Assessing Your Baseline of Multicultural Awareness

Multiculturalism as a field of study includes a complex array of issues, ideas, concepts, and beliefs. There are many closely related terms and concepts that are used every day but that are often somewhat overlapping and confusing. Also, in that we all live in a world comprised of a diversity of peoples, we develop a diversity of responses to those we interact with; that is, with some we know more accurately how to communicate, with others (usually those we have had less contact with) we often experience difficulty in establishing the same high level of communication as with those we more frequently associate with. The following two exercises help you self-assess your level of understanding of knowledge of and skill in multiculturalism. Both exercises in this activity (I-1) will help you assess your "beginning" baseline of attitude, knowledge, and skill in multiculturalism.

A. Warm-Up Exercise

There are many terms and concepts related to understanding multicultural issues. Often confusion, misunderstanding, and misuse of such terms occur when they have overlapping or similar meaning.

This exercise is intended to help you become aware of the meanings of some of the important terms and concepts related to multicultural relationships.

Match the terms and concepts below with the definitions on the facing page. An answer guide follows.

_____ 1. melting pot

_____ 2. Americanization

_____ 3. cultural pluralism

_____ 4. cultural universal

_____ 5. cultural relativity

_____ 6. values

_____ 7. cultural standards

_____ 8. liberal vs. conservative

_____ 9. White supremacy

_____ 10. races

_____ 11. racism

_____ 12. individual racism

_____ 13. institutional racism

_____ 14. cultural racism

_____ 15. racial minority

_____ 16. oppressed minority

_____ 17. ethnic minority

_____ 18. Third World

_____ 19. ethnocentrism

_____ 20. prejudice

_____ 21. discrimination

_____ 22. self-fulfilling prophecy

_____ 23. time orientation

_____ 24. psychodynamic issue

_____ 25. sociodynamic issue

_____ 26. synergetic

A. Virulent expression of White ethnocentrism.

B. Influence in the culture on thoughts, feelings, and behaviors toward experiencing of past, present, and future events.

C. People living in, or whose origins can be traced to, nations that are emerging (developing) as more technical and complex organizations.

D. Fusion of multicultures with a dominant culture.

E. Scientific classification as *Homo sapiens* into four groups of people.

F. Trends of sociopolitical beliefs and actions that might prevail in a society.

G. Belief that one's own group is the center of everything and all others are rated in reference to it.

H. Groups of people identified by national origins.

I. Personal issues that have become internalized within the personality.

J. Unity in diversity through coexistence.

K. Judging behavior in relation to the context of the group in which it occurs.

L. Issues that result from frustration in living in the society.

M. Differences based on racial preconceptions that may perpetuate inequality and that have become incorporated into the formal organized structure of the society over the years.

N. Status and freedom of a minority group is denied in comparison to the majority group.

O. Assimilation of multicultures into a dominant culture.

P. Treatment based on sex, age, race, religion, physical characteristics, national origins, or other distinguishing characteristics rather than qualifications.

Q. Prejudgment that does not take into consideration the actual realities or other aspects of a person, group, or situation.

R. Commonly held concepts and beliefs across different cultural groups.

S. Belief that some races are inherently superior to others.

T. Making beliefs or thoughts become real.

U. Thoughts, feelings, and behaviors by the members of a cultural group that their accomplishments are superior to that of other groups based on the racial composition of groups.

V. Thoughts, feelings, and behaviors shown by groups of people or individuals toward important objects of attention.

W. Thoughts, feelings, and behaviors of superiority by an individual based on racial background in relation to others who are viewed as inferior.

X. Groups of people who have become identified through distinctive physical characteristics or presumed inherited traits.

Y. Accepted standards of thoughts, feelings, and behaviors that a cultural group has developed over time.

Z. Working together of ideas from a variety of sources.

Answer Guide

_D_	1. melting pot	_U_	14. cultural racism
_O_	2. Americanization	_X_	15. racial minority
_J_	3. cultural pluralism	_N_	16. oppressed minority
_R_	4. cultural universal	_H_	17. ethnic minority
_K_	5. cultural relativity	_C_	18. Third World
_V_	6. values	_G_	19. ethnocentrism
_Y_	7. cultural standards	_O_	20. prejudice
_F_	8. liberal vs. conservative	_P_	21. discrimination
_A_	9. White supremacy	_T_	22. self-fulfilling prophecy
_E_	10. races	_B_	23. time orientation
_S_	11. racism	_I_	24. psychodynamic issue
_W_	12. individual racism	_L_	25. sociodynamic issue
_M_	13. institutional racism	_Z_	26. synergetic

1. Choose any five terms with their corresponding definition and discuss them with someone of a different ethnicity or race (or other nature of difference).

2. Are there differences of opinion or definition?

3. What did you learn by this discussion?

   a. Specifically:

   b. In general:

B. Multicultural Awareness/Knowledge/Skills Survey (MAKSS)

Complete the following survey. There are no correct answers; you are assessing only some of your current level of understanding in multiculturalism. At the end of this manual and after completing the exercises, it is helpful to complete the MAKSS instrument once again. This repetition may provide you a basic measure of what changes may have occurred in your attitude, knowledge, and/or skill foundations.

NOTE: After completion of the next several exercises in this section, it may be worthwhile to return to a discussion of the MAKSS topics and the thoughts it has stimulated.

THE MULTICULTURAL AWARENESS/KNOWLEDGE/SKILLS SURVEY (MAKSS)[1]

Here are a variety of issues related to the field of multicultural counseling and human services. Please read each statement/question carefully. From the available choices, check the one that best fits your reaction to each statement/question.

Note that each of the following questions may be potent content for a discussion group and/or be used as the theme of a written reaction to the topic. Such discussions and/or reaction paper might then be reexamined at the end of a course of study of such issues or after completing this manual.

1. Culture is not external but is within the person.   Not Sure   Strongly Disagree   Disagree   Agree   Strongly Agree
2. One of the potential negative consequences about gaining information concerning specific cultures is that students might stereotype members of those cultural groups according to the information they have gained.   Not Sure   Strongly Disagree   Disagree   Agree   Strongly Agree
3. At this time in your life, how would you rate yourself in terms of understanding how your cultural background has influenced the way you think and act?   Not Sure   Very Limited   Limited   Fairly Aware   Very Aware
4. At this point in your life, how would you rate your understanding of the impact of the way you think and act when interacting with persons of different cultural backgrounds?   Not Sure   Very Limited   Limited   Fairly Aware   Very Aware

Source: From "Evaluating the Impact of Multicultural Counseling Training" by M. D'Andrea, J. Daniels, and R. Heck, 1991, *Journal of Counseling and Development, 70*, pp. 149–150. Copyright 1991 by American Counseling Association. Reprinted by permission.
[1]Information on the MAKSS can be requested from Dr. Michael D'Andrea, University of Hawaii at Manoa, Honolulu, HI 96822.

5. How would you react to the following statement? While counseling enshrines the concepts of freedom, rational thought, tolerance of new ideas, and equality, it has frequently become a form of oppression to subjugate large groups of people.

Not Sure   Strongly Disagree   Disagree   Agree   Strongly Agree

6. In general, how would you rate your level of awareness regarding different cultural institutions and systems?

Not Sure   Very Limited   Limited   Fairly Aware   Very Aware

7. The human services professions, especially counseling and clinical psychology, have failed to meet the mental health needs of ethnic minorities.

Not Sure   Strongly Disagree   Disagree   Agree   Strongly Agree

8. At the present time, how would you generally rate yourself In terms of being able to accurately compare your own cultural perspective with that of a person from another culture?

Not Sure   Very Limited   Limited   Good   Very Good

9. How well do you think you could distinguish "intentional" from "accidental" communication signals in a multicultural counseling situation?

Not Sure   Very Limited   Limited   Good   Very Good

10. Ambiguity and stress often result from multicultural situations because people are not sure what to expect from each other.

Not Sure   Strongly Disagree   Disagree   Agree   Strongly Agree

11. The effectiveness and legitimacy of the counseling profession would be enhanced if counselors consciously supported universal definitions of normality.

Not Sure   Strongly Disagree   Disagree   Agree   Strongly Agree

12. The criteria of self-awareness, self-fulfillment, and self-discovery are important measures in most counseling sessions.

Not Sure   Strongly Disagree   Disagree   Agree   Strongly Agree

13. Even in multicultural counseling situations, basic implicit concepts, such as "fairness" and "health," are not difficult to understand.

Not Sure   Strongly Disagree   Disagree   Agree   Strongly Agree

14. Promoting a client's sense of psychological independence is usually a safe goal to strive for in most counseling situations.

Not Sure   Strongly Disagree   Disagree   Agree   Strongly Agree

15. While a person's natural support system (i.e., family, friends, etc.) plays an important role during a period of personal crisis, formal counseling services tend to result in more constructive outcomes.

Not Sure   Strongly Disagree   Disagree   Agree   Strongly Agree

16. How would you react to the following statement? In general, counseling services should be directed toward assisting clients to adjust to stressful environmental situations.

Not Sure   Strongly Disagree   Disagree   Agree   Strongly Agree

17. Counselors need to change not just the content of what they think but also the way they handle this content if they are to accurately account for the complexity in human behavior.

Not Sure   Strongly Disagree   Disagree   Agree   Strongly Agree

18. Psychological problems vary with the culture of the client.

Not Sure   Strongly Disagree   Disagree   Agree   Strongly Agree

19. How would you rate your understanding of the concept of "relativity" in terms of the goals, objectives, and methods of counseling culturally different clients?

Not Sure   Very Limited   Limited   Good   Very Good

20. There are some basic counseling skills that are applicable to create successful outcomes regardless of the client's cultural background.

Not Sure   Strongly Disagree   Disagree   Agree   Strongly Agree

At the present time, how would you rate your own understanding of the following terms (21–32):

21. *Culture*

Not Sure   Very Limited   Limited   Good   Very Good

22. *Ethnicity*

Not Sure   Very Limited   Limited   Good   Very Good

23. *Racism*

   Not Sure   Very Limited   Limited   Good   Very Good

24. *Mainstreaming*

   Not Sure   Very Limited   Limited   Good   Very Good

23. *Prejudice*

   Not Sure   Very Limited   Limited   Good   Very Good

26. *Multicultural Counseling*

   Not Sure   Very Limited   Limited   Good   Very Good

27. *Ethnocentrism*

   Not Sure   Very Limited   Limited   Good   Very Good

28. *Pluralism*

   Not Sure   Very Limited   Limited   Good   Very Good

29. *Contact Hypothesis*

   Not Sure   Very Limited   Limited   Good   Very Good

30. *Attribution*

   Not Sure   Very Limited   Limited   Good   Very Good

31. *Transcultural*

   Not Sure   Very Limited   Limited   Good   Very Good

32. *Cultural Encapsulation*

   Not Sure   Very Limited   Limited   Good   Very Good

33. What do you think of the following statement? Witch doctors and psychiatrists use similar techniques.

   Not Sure   Strongly Disagree   Disagree   Agree   Strongly Agree

34. Differential treatment in the provision of mental health services is not necessarily thought to be discriminatory.

   Not Sure   Strongly Disagree   Disagree   Agree   Strongly Agree

35. In the early grades of formal schooling in the United States, the academic achievement of such ethnic minorities as African Americans, Hispanics, and Native Americans is close to parity with the achievement of White mainstream students.

    Not Sure   Strongly Disagree   Disagree   Agree   Strongly Agree

36. Research indicates that in the early elementary school grades girls and boys achieve about equally in mathematics and science.

    Not Sure   Strongly Disagree   Disagree   Agree   Strongly Agree

37. Most of the immigrant and ethnic groups in Europe, Australia, and Canada face problems similar to those experienced by ethnic groups in the United States.

    Not Sure   Strongly Disagree   Disagree   Agree   Strongly Agree

38. In counseling, clients from different ethnic/cultural backgrounds should be given the same treatment that White mainstream clients receive.

    Not Sure   Strongly Disagree   Disagree   Agree   Strongly Agree

39. The difficulty with the concept of "integration" is its implicit bias in favor of the dominant culture.

    Not Sure   Strongly Disagree   Disagree   Agree   Strongly Agree

40. Racial and ethnic persons are underrepresented in clinical and counseling psychology.

    Not Sure   Strongly Disagree   Disagree   Agree   Strongly Agree

41. How would you rate your ability to conduct an effective counseling interview with a person from a cultural background significantly different from your own?

    Not Sure   Very Limited   Limited   Good   Very Good

42. How would you rate your ability to effectively assess the mental health needs of a person from a cultural background significantly different from your own?

    Not Sure   Very Limited   Limited   Good   Very Good

43. How well would you rate your ability to distinguish "formal" and "informal" counseling strategies?

    Not Sure   Very Limited   Limited   Good   Very Good

44. In general, how would you rate yourself in terms of being able to effectively deal with biases, discrimination, and prejudices directed at you by a client in a counseling setting?

Not Sure   Very Limited   Limited   Good   Very Good

45. How well would you rate your ability to accurately identify culturally biased assumptions as they relate to the process of counseling?

Not Sure   Very Limited   Limited   Good   Very Good

46. How well would you rate your ability to discuss the role of "method" and "context" as they relate to the process of counseling?

Not Sure   Very Limited   Limited   Good   Very Good

47. In general, how would you rate your ability to accurately articulate a client's problem who comes from a cultural group significantly different from your own?

Not Sure   Very Limited   Limited   Good   Very Good

48. How well would you rate your ability to analyze a culture into its component parts?

Not Sure   Very Limited   Limited   Good   Very Good

49. How would you rate your ability to identify the strengths and weaknesses of psychological tests In terms of their use with persons from different cultural/ racial/ethnic backgrounds?

Not Sure   Very Limited   Limited   Good   Very Good

50. How would you rate your ability to critique multicultural research?

Not Sure   Very Limited   Limited   Good   Very Good

51. In general, how would you rate your skill level in terms of being able to provide appropriate counseling services to culturally different clients?

Not Sure   Very Limited   Limited   Good   Very Good

52. How would you rate your ability to consult effectively with another mental health professional concerning the mental health needs of a client whose cultural background is significantly different from your own?

Not Sure   Very Limited   Limited   Good   Very Good

53. How would you rate your ability to effectively secure information and resources to better serve culturally different clients?

    Not Sure   Very Limited   Limited   Good   Very Good

54. How would you rate your ability to assess accurately the mental health needs of women?

    Not Sure   Very Limited   Limited   Good   Very Good

55. How would you rate your ability to assess accurately the mental health needs of men?

    Not Sure   Very Limited   Limited   Good   Very Good

56. How well would you rate your ability to assess accurately the mental health needs of older adults?

    Not Sure   Very Limited   Limited   Good   Very Good

57. How well would you rate your ability to assess accurately the mental health needs of gay men?

    Not Sure   Very Limited   Limited   Good   Very Good

58. How well would you rate your ability to assess accurately the mental health needs of gay women?

    Not Sure   Very Limited   Limited   Good   Very Good

59. How well would you rate your ability to assess accurately the mental health needs of persons with handicaps?

    Not Sure   Very Limited   Limited   Good   Very Good

60. How well would you rate your ability to assess accurately the mental health needs of persons who come from very poor socioeconomic backgrounds?

    Not Sure   Very Limited   Limited   Good   Very Good

Opportunity to Contribute to Multicultural Research

You are encouraged to participate in a research effort exploring multiculturalism. If you have completed the MAKSS survey as a member of a group, we suggest that you might compare answers according to age, religion, ethnicity, gender, and so on. Any number of variables existing within the group could be explored and compared for significance. There are a large number of professional journals in the helping professions and related disciplines that might find your results interesting The authors would appreciate a copy of your findings if you choose to do so. Please send a copy of your report to: Patrick McGrath, Ed.D., National-Louis University, Evanston, IL 60201.

ACTIVITY I-2
Assumptions about Others: A Group Exercise

Without the benefit of discussion before or during this group exercise, participants are asked to explore the reasons and basis for assigning ethnic/racial/cultural identity to others. Questions after each step should be answered *before* going on to the next step. We suggest that groups of four persons (who do not know each other) be formed for this exercise in the first group meeting. You could also do this activity as an individual, simply by observing people you come in contact with in daily living. Of course, this might imply some degree of risking offending others as you ascertain the accuracy of your assumptions about those you have observed by engaging them in a discussion.

After completing the activity, a discussion of the rationale and information used by each participant to assign identity to others is encouraged.

Record your answers for Steps A, B, C, and D in the chart below.

	STEP A	STEP B	STEP C	STEP D
Identity A				
Identity B				
Identity C				
Identity D				

Step A

Each person in the group is to make his or her *best guess* as to what cultural, racial, or ethnic group the other three persons belong. Record your answers under the Step A column in the chart. Remember who your three persons are by working from left to right (clockwise).

1. What primary information did you use in your decision to assign each particular identity? List the information.

A. _____

B. _____

C. _____

Step B

Now all participants prominently display their first name only. After participants have written and displayed their first name, reassess your best guess of Step A. Would you like to change your guess? Whether changed or not, record your answers under Step B in the chart.

2. Do first names influence you? Do they give you a clue? How are they useful to you? If you had only someone's first name (no visual contact), do you think you might guess that person's cultural, racial, or ethnic identity? Have others ever "identified" you based on your first name? What was that experience like? How did it affect you?

_____

_____

_____

_____

_____

_____

Step C

Now all participants share their last name by which they are currently, legally identified. Would you *now* like to change your guess? Whether changed or not, record your answer under Step C in the chart.

3. Do last names help you? Would this information have helped in accurately assigning identity? What most common mistake might still be made? Has your own last name undergone any changes of spelling or pronunciation that might mislead others? What are people's reactions to being culturally "identified" or categorized by their last name?

_____

_____

_____

_____

_____

Step D

Now all participants share the family name by which they were known as a child. For the three persons you identified, would you now like to change your guess? Whether changed or not, record your answers under Step D in the chart.

4. How are surnames useful? Can they confuse us? Have you ever received mail that is directed to you because your last name sounds like you are a member of a particular cultural group? If you are female (or male), what happens to personal identity and/or family and cultural identity when names are changed? Has this ever upset you?

    _____

    _____

    _____

    _____

    _____

    _____

In summary, answer the following questions.

a. How accurate were you? What prompted any changes?

b. What characteristics or information remained constant and thus assisted you in making accurate (or inaccurate) choices?

c. Without visual contact, what mistakes might have been made based on name alone?

d. Record any significant experiences/information shared by participants.

e. What have you discovered in this activity?

ACTIVITY I-3
Getting in Touch with Your Own Values

Values

Interpersonal and intergroup relations are influenced by people's perceptions of others. Values, as part of our internal selves, often structure *and* delimit our perceptions. They have influenced our course in the past, and are influencing it today. They help explain our nature and our behavior. What we value can be an idea, belief, practice, or anything that is important to us or anything that is desired. Values are also influenced by normative rules of conduct external to us and constitute the things we hold in common as members of a group, a culture, or a whole society. The way that certain common basic needs are satisfied and how values are defined tend to be related to such group membership. Values are conceptions that are explicitly or implicitly distinctive in an individual and may also be characteristic of a group. They constitute what is considered desirable and influence the selection of our behavior toward others. Values, as contained in our mind and emotions, can be measured through our personal evaluations or feelings about something.

FOR YOUR CONSIDERATION

Assume that all the cultures around the world could agree upon a set of just 20 values as encompassing all the values of humanity. Do you think each group would rank order these 20 values in the same sequence of priority—that is, assuming that "individualism" is valued, do you think it is *equally* valued by every culture? Might there be a differential in the rankings from group to group? Now, if there might be a difference in ranking, does that suggest that a value might fluctuate in meaning or "influence" upon individual or group behavior from culture to culture? Lastly, would any of these 20 values be likely to be "thrown off" a particular culture's list, or would it still be important, though perhaps not quite as important as another culture might think it to be?

Evaluating Your Personal Values

Column A

Rank in order of their importance to you the 20 values listed on the chart on page 22. Place a 1 in the A column across from the value that is *most* important to you. Place a 2 in the A column across from the value that is *second most* important to you, and so on. Complete column A *before* going on to B.

MYSELF		VALUES	OTHERS		SOCIETY
A	B		C	D	E
		Comfort			
		Equality			
		Excitement			
		Family security			
		Freedom			
		Inner harmony			
		Intimacy with spouse or partner			
		Pleasure			
		Variety			
		Regular routine			
		Self-respect			
		Sense of spiritual well-being (religious)			
		Sense of accomplishment			
		Social status			
		True friendship			
		Wisdom			
		National security (patriotism)			
		A world of peace and beauty			
		Group loyalty			
		Material success			

Column B

Select any group that you consider *culturally different* from your own, but this time rank the values *according to what you believe* might be the order of importance for members of that group. Make your arrangements in the B column next to the value. If you're not sure of a certain value, place a question mark in the space. Any one of the following groups or others not listed can be considered. Circle or identify the group selected.

Anglo-Saxon American   African American   Asian American

White Ethnic American   Hispanic American   Native American

Column C

Ask a person of the *different* group selected in column B also to rank order the 20 values in column C. Do not show your ranking.

Column D

In column D, ask a third person you consider culturally different from both of you also to rank order the 20 values. What is that person's identity?

_____

Column E

What do you think the general society of the United States would rank as the 5 most important values? Rank order these in column E.

Some Discussion Questions You Might Want to Pursue

1. What important values have you discovered in yourself?

2. What roles or functions do the values play in your personal life? In your relations with others?

3. Compare your top 5 ranked values with the other two persons' top 5 values as well as the general society's top 5 values.

	Yours	1st Person's	2nd Person's	General Society's
1				
2				
3				
4				
5				

4. Are there differences between each person's top 5? Between any individual's top 5 and your estimate of society's top 5? What do these differences suggest to you?

5. Do you believe that your perception of another cultural group's values (column B) is accurate? How did you arrive at your perceptions? Through general knowledge? experience? acquaintances? intuition? imagination?

6. If you left any question marks, can you determine anything from them?

7. What have you discovered about who is similar to whom? About values that may be common to people of different cultural backgrounds?

ACTIVITY I-4
How Do You Relate to Various Groups of People in the Society?

The purpose of the following list of individuals is to help you determine how you might respond at different levels to different persons. The levels of response are defined below. Try to respond as you honestly feel, not as you think might be considered socially or professionally desirable. Your answers are only for your own personal use in clarifying your initial reactions toward different people. You can substitute other categories of people "types" according to your work experience, community setting, or the like. For example, Haitian American could be substituted for any of items 1, 6, 11, 16, 21, or 26, or Baptist could be substituted for Islamic fundamentalist (28), or Prostitute for Homeless person (12).

Directions

Take one level of response at a time and follow it through the complete list of individuals in the left column. Place a check mark (✓) in the proper column only if you would answer NO *or if you hesitate before answering YES.* Quickly go through the complete list of individuals using response Level 1, then repeat with Level 2, and so on.

Levels of Response

1. I feel I can *greet* this person warmly and welcome him or her sincerely. If NO, place a check mark in column 1 of level of response columns.

2. I feel I can honestly *accept* this person as she or he is and be *comfortable* enough to listen to her or his problems. If NO, place a check mark in column 2.

3. I feel I would genuinely try to *help* the person with his or her problems as they might relate to or arise from the label-stereotype given to him or her here. If NO, place a check mark in column 3.

4. I feel I have the *background* of knowledge and/or experience to be able to help this person. If NO, place a check mark in column 4.

5. I feel I could honestly be an *advocate* for this person. If NO, place a check mark in column 5.

Check for NO answers only	LEVEL OF RESPONSE				
INDIVIDUAL	1 Greet	2 Accept	3 Help	4 Background	5 Advocate
1. Italian American					
2. Child abuser	✓		✓ →		✓
3. Jew					

Check for NO answers only	LEVEL OF RESPONSE				
INDIVIDUAL	1 Greet	2 Accept	3 Help	4 Background	5 Advocate
4. Amputee			✓ →		
5. Neo-Nazi	✓		✓ →		✓
6. Mexican American					
7. Divorced person			✓ →		
8. Catholic					
9. Senile elderly person			✓ →		
10. Teamster Union member	✓		✓ →		✓
11. Native American			✓ →		
12. Homeless person			✓ →		✓
13. Jehovah's Witness			✓ →		
14. Cerebral palsied person					
15. Abortion rights activist					✓
16. Vietnamese American			✓ →		
17. Gay/lesbian					
18. Atheist			✓ →		✓
19. Blind person			✓ →		
20. Political correctness extremist			✓ →		✓
21. African American					
22. Unmarried pregnant teenager					
23. Protestant					
24. Person with AIDS			✓ →		
25. Skinhead	✓		✓ →		✓

Check for NO answers only	LEVEL OF RESPONSE				
INDIVIDUAL	1 Greet	2 Accept	3 Help	4 Background	5 Advocate
26. White Anglo-Saxon American					
27. Alcoholic			✓ →		✓
28. Islamic fundamentalist			✓ →		✓
29. Person with facial disfiguration			✓ →		
30. Pro-life proponent					✓

You have completed the previous chart to see if you have difficulty in working with specific clients at various levels. The 30 types of individuals can be grouped into five categories: ethnic/racial, social issues/problems, religious, physical/mental disability, and political/social. Transfer your check marks to the following form. If you have a concentration of checks within a specific category of individuals or at specific levels, this may indicate a conflict or lack of knowledge that could hinder you from rendering effective professional help.

	LEVEL OF RESPONSE				
INDIVIDUAL	1 Greet	2 Accept	3 Help	4 Background	5 Advocate
ETHNIC/RACIAL:					
1. Italian American					
6. Mexican American					
11. Native American				✓	
16. Vietnamese American				✓	
21. African American					
26. White Anglo-Saxon American					

INDIVIDUAL	LEVEL OF RESPONSE				
	1 Greet	2 Accept	3 Help	4 Background	5 Advocate
SOCIAL ISSUES/PROBLEMS:					
2. Child abuser	✓			✓	✓
7. Divorced person				✓	
12. Homeless person				✓	✓
17. Gay/lesbian					
22. Unmarried pregnant teenager					
27. Alcoholic				✓	✓
RELIGIOUS:					
3. Jew					
8. Catholic					
13. Jehovah's Witness				✓	
18. Atheist				✓	✓
23. Protestant					
28. Islamic fundamentalist				✓	
PHYSICAL/MENTAL DISABILITY:					
4. Amputee				✓	
9. Senile elderly person				✓	
14. Cerebral palsied person					
19. Blind person				✓	
24. Person with AIDS				✓	
29. Person with facial disfiguration				✓	

INDIVIDUAL	LEVEL OF RESPONSE				
	1 Greet	2 Accept	3 Help	4 Background	5 Advocate
POLITICAL/SOCIAL:					
5. Neo-Nazi	✓			✓	✓
10. Teamster Union member	✓			✓	✓
15. Abortion rights activist					✓
20. Political correctness extremist				✓	✓
25. Skinhead	✓			✓	✓
30. Pro-life proponent					✓

Questions for Your Consideration

1. Is there a particular category of people or level of response that may present a conflict/difficulty for you? Identify.

2. What could you do to reduce such difficulty; that is, how could you improve your level of rendering effective professional help? *Social/political*

3. If you have a single group or category of groups that you *do not* believe you could work with,

   a. Clarify your reasons. *None*

   b. How would you refer a person from this group for help? To whom/where?

   ———————————

4. If you have strong perceptions (thoughts and/or feelings) about a particular grouping, you might consider what sources within your own culture and/or the society reinforce those perceptions. How and by what means does such reinforcement occur? How easy or difficult do you think it would be to change one's opinion in the face of such influence? What might be the potential risk of such a change in perception?

5. Would it be likely for you to find work in a counseling agency/role in which you would be assigned the kind of client you don't like to (or "can't") work with? What would you do?

ACTIVITY I-5
An Assessment of Multicultural Contacts

Our ability to relate effectively to any event or person we experience is influenced by the *quantity* as well as the *quality* of experiences we have had with similar events or persons. Based on both the quality and quantity of such exposure, we often develop a reservoir of information and ways of relating to such people and events.

For example, we may have had some level of significant contact with three persons of Asian heritage. From this limited sample we may develop perceptions of Asians that influence future contacts with other Asians. Let us assume one contact involved an argument over an item to be purchased; do we judge what occurred to be generalized to all Asians? What if all three contacts were similar (e.g., involved arguments)? Can we now validly generalize that Asians are argumentative? To be a valid generalization, with how many Asians must we have had this experience? Or does this experience say more about ourselves than it might say about Asians?

In this exercise you will examine the frequency and nature of significant contacts with those who are culturally different from yourself. Such characteristics as skin color or physical features or even language should not limit your choices. List any person(s) who, in your own mind, you identify as culturally different. For example, would you consider Irish persons to be different from Swedes? from Mexicans? from Puerto Ricans? from Japanese? Could you look at gender differences or age differences in similar fashion? In a global sense, are Africans (nationals from Africa) different from African Americans?

Note that "significant contact" is taken to mean that for some reason you can recall that the contact meant more to you than just simply "passing someone by" on the street.

1. List different cultural groups with which you have had significant contact. Such contacts may have occurred at school, work, vacation, public events, and so on. The contact may involve meeting only one or several representatives of that group. Fill in the chart columns below with the designated information.

    For example, in column 1 list the different cultural groups with which you have had significant contact. In column 2 list how many different individuals of this group you have had contact with. In column 3 list the frequency of contact—that is, how many times the contact occurred: once a week, once a day, once only. In column 4 list unique or noted differences between you and the cultural group. And in column 5 list any noted similarities between you and the group.

Chart A: Contact with Other Cultural Groups

	1	2	3	4	5
1.					
2.					
3.					
4.					
5.					
6.					

2. Does it surprise you how many or how few cross-cultural contacts you have had?

3. What accounts for the frequency of these contacts? Without being fully aware, or by purposefully being aware, have you determined the frequency of contact by acting to seek out or to avoid persons of different cultural heritages?

4. Does the location of your residence or work or personal choices influence the frequency of contact? In what ways?

5. Without frequency of personal contact, how can people expand their understandings of culturally different others? Also, can frequency of contact with a person particularly disagreeable to us influence our perceptions or behavior toward other members of that same group? Explain.

6. What other avenues to cultural awareness exist and how valid do you think they might be to you? What concerns would you have about expanding your awareness of other cultural groups?

7. What concerns would you have if your awareness of different cultures were based only on personal contacts with individuals of that different culture?

8. Now reflect on your contacts with specific individuals from any two of the culture groups listed in Chart A. For example, if you have met three different persons of Hungarian heritage, list each person on Chart B and complete the column answers below; then do the same for another group of two or more. Note that the interpersonal nature of each contact may be of great importance to your perceptions of difference or similarity, interest or disinterest, concern or nonconcern about a particular cultural group that is different from your own cultural group.

Chart B: Experiences with Members of the Same Cultural Group

DIFFERENT CULTURE (persons from same group)	FREQUENCY OF CONTACT (how many times)	NATURE OF CONTACT	NOTED DIFFERENCE	NOTED SIMILARITY
Group One Person 1. Person 2. Person 3.				

DIFFERENT CULTURE (persons from same group)	FREQUENCY OF CONTACT (how many times)	NATURE OF CONTACT	NOTED DIFFERENCE	NOTED SIMILARITY
Group Two Person 1. Person 2. Person 3.				

9. After completing Chart B and reviewing what you wrote about the group of individuals of the specific different cultures and the nature of your contacts, would you change any of your answers to questions that you previously answered (questions 1–7)?

10. What might you surmise about individual difference among members of the same cultural group?

11. Given your different cultural contacts (Chart A):

    a. Which group is *most* similar to your own culture? _____

    b. Which group is *most* different from your own culture? _____

12. Which of your identified culture groups (Chart A) would you place together as similar to each other but different from another group? Write your responses below.

		SIMILAR	DIFFERENT
Example:	Korean	Chinese	African
Group:			

13. Which groups would you place together as *similar to each other* but *most different* from your own cultural group?

		My Group
Group:		

14. Which groups would you place together *as similar to each other* and *most similar* to your own group?

		My Group
Group:		

15. Does the similarity/dissimilarity of other cultural groups to your own cultural group in any way account for the frequency of contacts you have had with such groups? Are there any other explanations for your high or low frequency of contact with different cultural groups?

ACTIVITY I-6
What It Is Like to Be a Person of a Different Cultural (or Subcultural) Heritage

Essay on being _____ .

1. Write a one- or two-page essay on what it is like to be a person with a different racial/ethnic/cultural background (or other nature of differentness). For example, if you are a White Ethnic American, what is it like to be an African American; if you are an African American, what is it like to be an Asian American; if you are 25 years old, what is it like to be 80 years old; if you have your hearing, what is it like to be deaf?

2. If it is possible, share your essay with (a) another person of your own background and (b) someone of the background you wrote about.
   Note: If possible, choose people who are close friends to you.

3. What were their reactions? Was your essay: very descriptive? somewhat descriptive? not descriptive at all? stereotypical or prejudicial?

4. What did you discover about your perceptions and understanding of different others?

5. What did you discover about yourself'?

_____

FOR YOUR CONSIDERATION
Since within-group differences may often be greater (more variable) than between-group differences, it may be valuable to establish a panel of respondents comprised of members of the group you wrote your essay on. What similar as well as dissimilar reactions are there to your essay?

_____

ACTIVITY I-7
Identifying Sources of Multicultural Information

1. List several sources from which you have obtained information of a multicultural nature. How accurate would you estimate the cultural information is in these sources? Would you say: highly accurate? somewhat accurate? not very accurate? Ask several culturally different people what their estimate is of the accuracy of the cultural information contained in these sources.

SOURCE	YOUR ESTIMATE OF CULTURAL ACCURACY	OTHERS' ESTIMATE OF CULTURAL ACCURACY
1.		
2.		
3.		
4.		
5.		
6.		
7.		
8.		

2. What do your colleagues or culturally different others think of the accuracy, reliability, and so on of such sources of information?

SUMMARY OF SECTION I
Influences from and Understandings of Cross-Cultural Experiences

Return to the information you examined in the MAKSS instrument and Activities I-1 through I-7. Try to identify the most critical ideas relevant to:

1. Your self-identity.

2. Your cross-cultural experiences.

3. Your frequency of contacts with different cultures.

4. Expanding your multicultural knowledge.

5. List what one ought to be cautious about (e.g., avoiding assumptions) when trying to expand one's multicultural understanding.

6. Based on your work in Section I, what message, idea, perception about multiculturalism would you like to identify to yourself or to a group of your colleagues at this time?

II

Cultural Self-Awareness

Background Reading: Chapter 2, "The Culture of the Counselor," in John A. Axelson, *Counseling and Development in a Multicultural Society* (3rd ed.). Pacific Grove, Calif.: Brooks/Cole, 1999.

FOR YOUR CONSIDERATION

We might imagine that we are each the product of a "cultural learning box"; that is, we develop in interaction with the life experiences that have been and are presented to us in the surrounding environment. And we all live, grow, and develop within a variety of such learning boxes. Of course, some experiences within these learning environments mute or blunt others. Nevertheless, family is often the first of many such learning environments—and it is often the most powerful and longest lasting among them.

Each person brings a variety of understandings and experiences to a relationship. Much of this information was developed within the framework of family experiences. Other significant information was obtained during relationships with other persons and events in the society as well as from changing social and world conditions.

While there is powerful, theoretical (abstract) knowledge to guide us in effecting therapeutic relationships, self-awareness of the kinds of unique personal and cultural influences operating upon our self is most critical. In a helping relationship, such personal influences interact with similar personal influences operating on the client. Awareness of the interaction of these needs, beliefs, ideas, behaviors, attitudes, biases, prejudices, and ignorances with theoretical knowledge of the context of human relationships is critical. How well we understand our own needs and goals within a relationship will determine, to a great extent, the outcomes of that relationship regardless of the nature of the contact.

Our self- and cultural-awareness, our awareness of clients' own uniqueness and culture, and our awareness of their interaction within and upon the immediate relationship are all necessary to finding successful solutions. Thus, to recognize the dynamic, constant influence cultures have on human actions and reactions is an important goal.

For example, imagine a soccer team composed of star players brought together from different countries, each with his or her own language and thought processes. Even assuming that all would learn a common language and that each player possesses an equally high-level skill and understanding of the game, the team may not necessarily be successful initially. That is, under the stress of competition, each player might resort to thinking and making decisions in his or her language of origin as well as according to the strategy of the game as learned in the player's country of origin (i.e., the English may approach the game differently than the Brazilians). Perhaps a slight difference in the amount of time required to translate cognitively from one's own language and learned strategies to the new shared language may cause a disjointed rather than synchronized effort to score a goal. However, we may assume that practice (i.e., frequency of contact) encourages awareness and adaptation to the thought processes and strategy choices of the other players. Contact, per se, may encourage the synchronization of team member efforts and lead to increasingly successful teamwork.

In a similar vein, professional helping also requires synchronized teamwork between the helper and client. The nature of a successful relationship requires each participant, albeit in each's own manner and own pace, to be aware of self and of the other. The choice of achievable goals, of useful strategies, and of appropriate techniques is quite dependent upon shared understanding.

The sharing of information necessary to creating effective interactions is influenced by the values and beliefs we have. When there are clear differences in value orientations between persons, such differences may be major obstacles to the relationship. Understanding our values and how they may be different from another's often helps us to discover how to improve the relationship.

ACTIVITY II-1
United States Value Orientation[1]

The following exercise asks you to assess your adherence to hypothesized U.S. values relative to other countries' values. On each of the 13 following continuums of values, identify which end of the continuum you tend to agree with or believe in more strongly. Indicate the strength of your beliefs by circling the number on the continuum closest to where you now are on the continuum. Certainly we might appreciate the values hypothesized on *each end* of the continuum. Nevertheless, the manner in which we live our lives often suggests or identifies what we most value as we compare/contrast the end points of any continuum.

---

[1]Adapted from the work of Robert Kohl, Washington International Center, Washington, D.C.

U.S. VALUES   OTHER COUNTRIES' VALUES

Control over Environment --- Fate

1   2   3   (4)   5   6   7   8   9   10

Change --- Tradition

1   2   3   (4)   5   6   7   8   9   10

                                               Time Schedules Secondary
Time Control --to Relationships

1   2   3   4   5   6   (7)   8   9   10

Equality-- Hierarchy/Rank/Status

1   2   3   (4)   5   6   7   8   9   10

Individualism/Privacy -- Group's Welfare

1   (2)   3   4   5   6   7   8   9   10

Self-Reliance---Group Aid

1   2   3   4   (5)   6   7   8   9   10

Competition --Cooperation

1   2   3   4   5   (6)   7   8   9   10

Future Orientation --- Past Orientation

1   2   3   4   (5)   6   7   8   9   10

Action/Activity Oriented------------------------------------- Taking Time to Reflect

1   2   3   4   5   (6)   7   8   9   10

Informality --Formality

1   2   (3)   4   5   6   7   8   9   10

Directness/Openness ------------------------------------- Indirectness/Ritualization

1   (2)   3   4   5   6   7   8   9   10

Practicality/Efficiency --- Idealism

1   2   3   4   (5)   6   7   8   9   10

Materialism/Acquiring ----------------------------------- Spiritualism/Detachment

1   2   (3)   4   5   6   7   8   9   10

Some Questions/Ideas to Consider

1. According to your score average, how "USA-ized" are you? _4.4_

2. Do you think your "fit" on any one, as well as all the continuums together, increases or decreases the likelihood that value differences may be a problem as related to communicating with someone having a different "fit"?

3. Which of the values do you consider to be the most dominant influence in your life? _Individualism / Openness_

4. Can you identify any particular culture(s) that you believe hold opposite values and that you believe would be the most difficult to work with (for you)?

5. Are there any other value continuums you would suggest for this exercise?

6. If possible, ask several persons from other countries to identify:

   a. What they believe people in the United States value.

   b. What they themselves value.

   What have you become aware of as you compare the responses?

ACTIVITY II-2
What Do You Believe about the Human Experience?

Culture is an expression of how over time and over the world people have learned to view the human experience. Worldviews can be related to five basic philosophical components of the human experience:

1. Human nature.

2. Human activity.

3. Relations with the physical (natural) world.

4. Relationship with the self.

5. Relationship with others.

This activity is intended to assist you in discovering and learning more about your view of the world according to these five components.

A. Basic Components of Human Experience: An Exercise in Sorting Out Contrasting Cultural Views

Directions:

For each of the following 33 statements, determine which one of the two contrasting descriptions of cultural values and practices you lean toward. *Circle only one number for each statement* (3 = strong belief, 2 = some belief, 1 = little or no belief,

0 = no answer, meaning you do not know or it is impossible for you to determine). Thus, for the first statement, if you circled 3 on the right side, you strongly believe that innate human nature is evil; whereas if you circled 2 on the left side, you believe somewhat that innate nature is good. Remember, you rate only the value or practice that you lean *toward*.

HUMAN NATURE		
1. Innate human nature is:		
good	(3) 2 1 0 1 2 3	evil
constructive	(3) 2 1 0 1 2 3	destructive
2. People:		
can control (master) human nature	3 2 1 (0) 1 2 3	are controlled (subjugated) by human nature
SUM =	6	
HUMAN ACTIVITY		
3. Activity is:		
concern with doing something, gaining something, progress, change, achievement, striving, optimistic	(3) 2 1 0 1 2 3	"being" spontaneous, expressing what happens will happen, accepting life as it flows, fatalistic
4. A desirable pace of life is:		
fast, busy, driving	(3) 2 1 0 1 2 3	steady, rhythmic, noncompulsive
5. The emphasis in planning activities is:		
the means, procedures, techniques	3 2 1 0 1 2 (3)	the final goal
6. Important goals in life are:		
material comfort and absence of pain, activity	3 2 1 0 1 (2) 3	spiritual, fullness of pain and pleasure, experience
7. Activity is evaluated on the basis of:		
utility and practicality (does it work?)	3 2 1 0 1 (2) 3	essence (is it ideal?)

8. Who should make decisions?		
the people affected	(3) 2 1 0 1 2 3	those with proper authority
9. What is learning activity?		
learner is active (learner-centered)	(3) 2 1 0 1 2 3	learner is passive (material-centered)
SUM =	7	

RELATIONS WITH PHYSICAL WORLD

10. Mind and body:		
exist separately	3 2 1 0 1 2 (3)	work together
11. People:		
control the physical world	(3) 2 1 0 1 2 3	are controlled by the physical world
12. The natural world:		
is physical and mechanical in which people make use of machines	3 (2) 1 0 1 2 3	is spiritual and organic (living) and disavows machines
13. The world operates in a:		
rational, learnable, controllable manner involving probability and predictability	3 (2) 1 0 1 2 3	mystically ordered, spiritually conceived manner involving divination, without predictability or probability
14. People:		
exist apart from nature or from any hierarchy in nature	3 2 1 0 1 (2) 3	are a part of nature or of some hierarchy
15. Good resources in nature are:		
unlimited and people should modify nature for their use	3 2 1 0 1 (2) 3	limited and people should accept the natural order
16. Truth and goodness are:		
found in the analysis of what works in each circumstance	3 2 1 (0) 1 2 3	absolute and apprehended as a whole
17. Property is:		
private ownership as extension of self	(3) 2 1 0 1 2 3	used for natural purposes regardless of ownership

18. Time is: work and anticipation of the future, measured in precise units, lineal, and a limited source SUM =	3 2 1 0 1 (2) 3 10 9	the past that is remembered, the present experienced, undifferentiated units, circular, and not limited
RELATIONSHIP WITH THE SELF		
19. The self is defined as: diffuse, changing, flexible (being-in-becoming)	(3) 2 1 0 1 2 3	fixed, clearly defined, located in a social system (being)
20. A person's identity is: within the self (achievement, etc.)	3 2 1 0 1 (2) 3	outside the self in roles, group, family, clan, caste, society
21. One's sense of responsibility rests in: the self	(3) 2 1 0 1 2 3	the group
22. One should place reliance on: self and impersonal organizations (job, government)	3 2 1 0 1 (2) 3	status, superiors, benefactor, kin, and other persons
23. The kind of person who is valued and respected is: one who is youthful (vigorous)	3 2 1 0 1 2 (3)	aged (wise, experienced)
24. Social control of behavior is based on: persuasion, appeal to the individual, guilt (blame)	3 (2) 1 0 1 2 3	formality, authority, shame
25. Responsibility for decisions: lies with each individual SUM=	3 2 1 0 1 2 (3) 8 10	is a function of a group or resides in the role the individual has

RELATIONSHIP WITH OTHERS		
26. The nature of relations is determined by: each individual (individualistic)	3 (2) 1 0 1 2 3	lineal ordering (submission to others by way of heredity, sex, age, ancestors)
27. The roles (parents, spouse, child, etc.) that one performs are: earned, loose, general	3 2 1 (0) 1 2 3	given, tight, specific
28. When people relate to others whose status and/or role is different: equality and informality should be emphasized and differences minimized	(3) 2 1 0 1 2 3	hierarchical ranks, formality, and differences should be emphasized
29. Sex roles should be: less legitimized, similar, overlapping, equal, with friends of both sexes	(3) 2 1 0 1 2 3	legitimized, distinct, unequal, male superiority, with friends of same sex only
30. In a group, a member's rights and duties should be to: assume limited liability, join to seek own goals, be active in order to influence group	(3) 2 1 0 1 2 3	assume unlimited liability accept constraint by group, let leader run group (members do not)
31. People judge others: by their specific abilities or interests (task, achievement)	(3) 2 1 0 1 2 3	by their overall individuality and status
32. Friendship is: social friendship (short-term commitments, friends are shared)	3 2 1 0 1 2 (3)	intense friendship (long-term commitment, friends are exclusive)
33. Friendly aggression in social interaction is: acceptable, interesting, fun SUM =	3 (2) 1 0 1 2 3 16 3	not acceptable, embarrassing
FINAL TOTAL SCORE	52 29 Left 0 Right	

36/52

B. What Is Your Worldview?

Add up your numbers for each cultural component and for your final total score.

	LEFT SIDE	UNDECIDED (number of 0s)	RIGHT SIDE
Human Nature	6	1	0
Human Activity	12		7
Relations with Physical (Natural) World	10	1	9
Relationship with the Self	8		10
Relationship with Others	16	1	3
FINAL TOTAL SCORE	52	3	29

Descriptions:

Left side: Higher scores as compared with those on the right side tend to represent mainstream United States culture: emphasis on competition and individualism, with internal locus of control and internal locus of responsibility.

Undecided: Marginal, undifferentiated area; this means you are unsure of your worldview, or in process of changing your worldview.

Right side: Higher scores as compared with those on the left side tend to represent a non–U.S. worldview: emphasis on cooperation and group orientation, with external locus of control and external locus of responsibility.

1. After viewing your scores, how would you describe your worldview?

2. You may want to compare your answers with others; or, when you are conducting cross-cultural interviews later in this manual, you can ask your interviewees to answer the "What Do You Believe about the Human Experience?" survey. Then compare their answers to yours. Are there any similarities? What areas are they in? Are there any differences? What areas are they in?

3. You might also ask other family members, particularly parents and siblings, to respond to these questions. Are there greater or lesser similarities in the worldview of "immediate" family members versus the extended family? of others who share your heritage? of others in the neighborhood? of others from different heritages?

ACTIVITY II-3
Stereotypes versus Reality

A stereotype is a generalized and usually quite simplified conceptualization or belief about another person or people, place, or thing. The use of stereotypes to identify and describe others is quite common, and stereotypes have a major influence upon our perception of others. The use of stereotypical statements to describe persons different from ourselves, particularly when not contradicted, reinforces already existing notions of the nature of other persons or groups. The use of stereotypes to identify others is complicated by possible elements of truthfulness in the description. The danger in a possible truthful part of a stereotypic description is that this truthful element often clouds the total picture. Nevertheless, many of us use stereotypical understandings of others to explain a variety of unique individual experiences with people who are different from ourselves.

Stereotypes are so commonly bandied about that we can easily begin to think they are true—simply because we have heard them so often. The old adage, "If you tell a person something often enough and loudly enough, that person will come to believe it" seems to hold true. Without sufficient experience with *others of difference,* it is very difficult for each of us to know what is usefully truthful and what is neither truthful nor useful (in understanding others). And, without corrective feedback, it is often difficult to know when we might be stereotyping another.

1. Can you identify any stereotyping associated with your own cultural heritage? List below the type of *general comments* that are made about your own culture. (This could be relative to one's identification as male/female, young/old, as well as one's ethnicity or race.)

   a. _____

   b. _____

   c. _____

   d. _____

2. Choose one or more cultural groups different from your own and identify common stereotypes associated with this group. List below the types of *general comments* that are made about this (these) other culture(s).

   a. _____

   b. _____

   c. _____

   d. _____

3. Take both lists and share them with a person or persons of your own heritage.

   a. What elements of any general comment were agreed with even if the entirety of the comment was disagreed with?

   b. What did they totally agree with?

   c. What did they totally disagree with?

4. Take both lists and share them with a person or persons of a different heritage.

   a. What elements of any general comment were agreed with even if the entirety of the comment was disagreed with?

   b. What did they totally agree with?

   c. What did they totally disagree with?

5. Can you identify what stereotypes you have formed about various groups, places, or things? List these below.

   a. People (groups):

   b. Places (nations or region of a country):

   c. Things (e.g., Miss America contest):

6. What have you discovered about stereotypes and stereotyping?

7. As a final exercise to explore stereotypical understandings, consider constructing your own survey form (an example is shown on page 47) regarding both truthful and nontruthful statements about your own culture. You might also construct a similar survey form regarding another culture. Ask any mixture of 10 persons or 10 persons of the same cultural group to answer your questions. Upon completing your research and analyzing the data, answer the following questions:

   a. What do the data indicate about respondents' answers?

   b. What do you think of this information? Were you surprised? Do you think most people think the same? What could be done to change perceptions or to correct incorrect perceptions, beliefs, attitudes?

   c. How powerful are stereotypes in influencing us?

   d. What is the most difficult aspect of stereotyping?

NOTE: Some misconceptions have been so overused or their inaccuracy is so well known that it is difficult to believe that they continue to linger in U.S. society. The statements listed in the sample questionnaire that follows have been (and possibly still are) commonly believed at one time or another in the history of this country. Except for the last item on the questionnaire, all these statements are false stereotypes that create confusion, misrepresent the character of the people, and are derogatory or degrading.

Sample Questionnaire on Stereotypes

STEREOTYPES VERSUS REALITY QUESTIONNAIRE

True	False	Not Sure/ No Answer	Native Americans:
_____	_____	_____	do not have the potential to understand relationships in a complex, technical modern society.
_____	_____	_____	are vanishing Americans.
_____	_____	_____	are illiterate and nonintellectual.
_____	_____	_____	are simple-minded people whose worship of nature is nonreligious.
_____	_____	_____	are good at working only with their hands, drawing pictures, arts and crafts, music, or repetitious factory work.
_____	_____	_____	are passive and primitive people who are ignorant of modern society.
_____	_____	_____	all follow the same traditions as do members of any homogeneous ethnic group.
_____	_____	_____	are romantic, childlike people who love nature.
_____	_____	_____	are noble savages.
_____	_____	_____	are members of many different tribes, thus constituting a multicultural Native American society.

ACTIVITY II-4
What Are Your Roots?

Tracing your own ancestral relationships and the patterns they follow can be a fascinating and broadening experience. For example, many Asian Americans believe in a concept of family that recognizes past and present kin. This concept leads to a timeless sense of bonding and identity with other significant people in one's family and may help to bring a deeper personal feeling of belonging and meaning in life. Your own careful genealogical research may enable you to trace your descent from at least some of your ancestors and eventually to draw an accurate family tree. Begin with yourself, your parents, and your grandparents, and then proceed as far back to other generations as possible.

What Is Important for You to Know?

1. What generation in the United States do you represent? Are you and your brothers and sisters the first members of your family to be born in this country?

2. How did your ancestors arrive in the United States? From where? For what reason(s)? Did you or your parents or grandparents have any particular difficulties in adjusting?

3. Does your immediate family or extended family practice ethnic or cultural customs that you or they value or identify with (for example: foods, celebrations, traditions, social behaviors, manners, beliefs)?

   a. What customs do you prize the most?

   b. Do you or your relatives speak a language different from standard English? Are you bilingual? If so, in what ways is this useful to you? If not, do you wish you were? Why or why not?

4. What social conditions or conflicts have you or your kin experienced within the present U.S. culture? In the past? What migration experiences do you or other members of your family remember?

5. What occupations are represented in your family background? Has each generation expected its children to "do better"? Is your present behavior in any way related to your ancestors' hopes and dreams?

Where You Can Get More Information

You can research your genealogy on whatever level you desire, but you must start at home and progress from recent ancestors to earlier ones. What history or experiences do you know or remember about your family? Oftentimes old records, letters, documents, and photos are available. Did you ever look at a family picture album and imagine what life was like to those in the photos? Try interviewing your parents and relatives for information about their life. How did they picture you when you were growing up? The "family voyage" will be a broadening trip for you.

If you really want to get into it, go to resources developed by various societies and organizations that compile family histories. Here are some lines of research you can try:

1. Cities and counties keep records of birth, marriages, and deaths. Church records are also valuable sources of information. The U.S. Census of 1790 recorded genealogical information.

2. Printed "pedigrees" of families are available in many public libraries and through the Library of Congress in Washington, D.C.; the Newberry Library in Chicago; the Henry E. Huntington Library in San Marino, California; and the New England Historical and Genealogical Society Library in Boston. The headquarters of the Mormon Church in Salt Lake City, Utah, has on computer thousands of family histories.

3. If you happen to take a trip overseas, you can find many groups to assist you in your search of family origins. In England, the Family Heritage Holidays prepares an entire trip to locate the town or village from which the traveler's ancestors came. Scotland operates the Clan Tartan Center, which uses a computer to trace a surname. The Irish Tourist Board also helps Americans with Irish surnames, and the Swedish town of Växjö, from which half of the people emigrated to the United States between 1850 and 1930, even has a House of Emigrants to which visitors can go to find their origins. Israel has many archives containing useful information. The computer in the Museum of the Jewish Diaspora in Tel Aviv contains much information about Jewish settlements. The Central Archives in Jerusalem is a valuable source for names and families and traces Jewish history from the 12th century.

4. A smoothly written and carefully researched book, *Coming to America: Immigrants from Eastern Europe,* by Shirley Blumenthal (New York: Delacorte, 1982), gives a lively account of the reasons for emigrating, problems encountered on the voyage, and the problems faced in a new land. It is geared to older children but appropriate for any age.

5. Viewing the film series *Roots* or reading the book *Roots,* by Alex Haley (New York: Dell, 1980), will sensitize you to the trauma of slavery that African Americans faced in the early history of the United States. You can also broaden your horizons by observing some of the events and contributions during the annual Black History/Heritage Month in February. The recognition and celebration of Black history originated in 1915 through the efforts of historian Carter G. Woodson, who believed that education in the history of one's group was essential to the preservation of the group.

6. The booklet, *Ellis Island: Gateway to America,* by Loretto Dennis Szucs (Salt Lake City: Ancestry, 1986), recalls the pain and excitement of immigration to the United States during the period from 1892 to the early 20th century. More than 12 million immigrants from Europe and other places had been processed through Ellis Island by the time it was closed in 1954. During the peak years from about 1900 to 1914, as many as five thousand people a day were processed. The publication also tells you how to find out if your ancestors came through Ellis Island and gives helpful lists of sources for genealogical research. Another reference, *Ellis Island: A Pictorial History*, by Barbara Benton (New York: Facts on File Publications, 1987), offers exceptional documentation and visual re-creation of the same time period.

7. Following is a "pedigree chart," or, if you prefer, a road map to your ancestors that you can use in getting started on your own genealogical search. You are letter *A* on the charts; your father is number two; and your mother is number three. Always place the males under the *even* numbers and the females under the *odd* numbers. Once you identify as many ancestors as you can, the challenge and fun of gathering information about them is the next step. Activities II-5 and II-6 will guide you.

8. Other good sources for cultural heritage information are university libraries and academic programs and departments such as cultural studies, history,

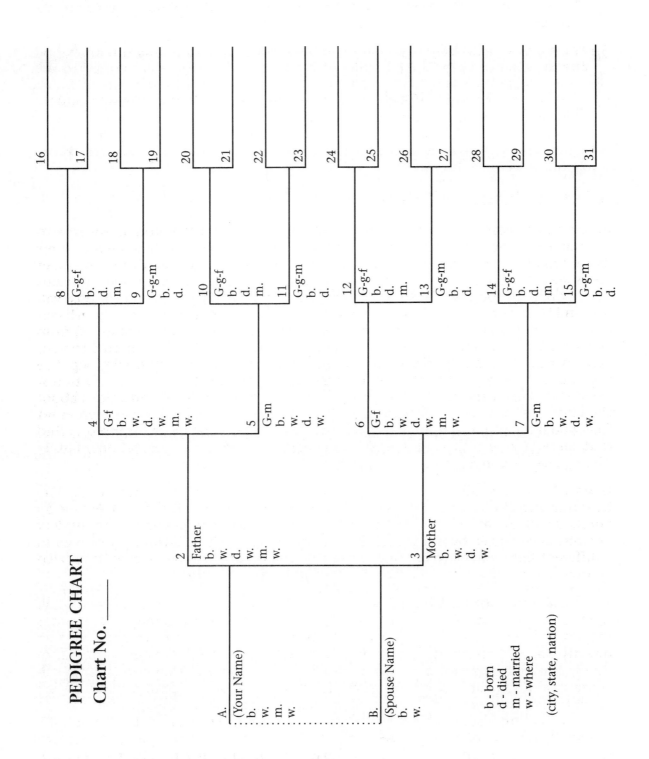

PEDIGREE CHART _____

Chart No. _____

A.
....
(Your Name)
b.
w.
m.
w.

B.
(Spouse Name)
b.
w.

2 Father
b.
w.
d.
w.
m.
w.

3 Mother
b.
w.
d.
w.

4 G-f
b.
w.
d.
w.
m.
w.

5 G-m
b.
w.
d.
w.

6 G-f
b.
w.
d.
w.
m.
w.

7 G-m
b.
w.
d.
w.

8 G-g-f
b.
d.
m.

9 G-g-m
b.
d.

10 G-g-f
b.
d.
m.

11 G-g-m
b.
d.

12 G-g-f
b.
d.
m.

13 G-g-m
b.
d.

14 G-g-f
b.
d.
m.

15 G-g-m
b.
d.

16

17

18

19

20

21

22

23

24

25

26

27

28

29

30

31

b - born
d - died
m - married
w - where

(city, state, nation)

anthropology, international studies, sociology, psychology, and counseling. These can often provide many relevant reference materials about your or others' heritage.

9. The embassy or consulate of your or your family's country of origin may also be a great help.

10. Other good sources are the plays, movies, books, and museums listed in Appendix A.

ACTIVITY II-5
A Family/Culture Interview

In order to explore your cultural heritage further, we suggest that you interview several relatives about your family and/or cultural history. If possible, include the oldest living relative. It is not uncommon that the oldest family member can remember and speak about a time when persons of your heritage group lived in homogeneous neighborhoods and there was less diversity (than tolerated today) about norms, values, and behaviors expected of group members. It may be possible to distinguish certain behaviors that tend to be culture specific and have also been transmitted from generation to generation. Remember, relatives' information is often specific to incidents within your family in addition to generalizations about the cultural group. Use the questions given in the "Family/Culture Questionnaire" that follows. Try to distinguish between specific family history and knowledge and generalizations about the culture as a whole. Personally recalled information does not always represent that which is culturally widespread. Nevertheless, you may be quite surprised to find that some of your beliefs, attitudes, and behaviors have a transgenerational family history *and are also* repeated throughout your cultural group.

Essentially, we are talking about historical data that may have relevance today. The introduction of ideas and behaviors and their subsequent daily reinforcement by family, relatives, and anyone throughout the culture are very powerful. The anxiety or stress experienced by individuals seeking to change their behavior may be seen in a different light when we become aware that the original behavior may have been approved and reinforced over the years by family and/or culture.

As an example, although marrying outside one's own culture or race may seem all right to the individuals, it may have a negative impact upon the family relationships they want to maintain. There may even be two families/cultures (each spouse's) that directly oppose this marriage and attempt to actively or passively undermine it. In times of need, one commonly turns to the family for support. If support is not forthcoming or if there are culturally held beliefs and behaviors concerning the "proper" resolution of such problems, the situation may be aggravated. An argument may be more difficult to resolve given a preferred "style of arguing" that has been culturally and familially reinforced over the years. It may be easy to misinterpret such learned styles of handling conflict as simply one partner's personal reaction to the other. For example, if expressing feelings is expected by one spouse (according to his or her cultural understandings) but is perceived as offensive by the other spouse (according to her or his culturally based style), it is helpful to determine whether this is a "clash" between different culture-based styles or is indeed a personal effort to further offend or anger the other.

Family/Culture Questionnaire

1. What is the average size and composition of the family in this culture?

2. What is the authority structure of the family in this culture?

3. What are the role concepts within the family in this culture?

4. Do family and cultural traditions have certain expectations of male and female members?

5. How are names chosen for family members? Is there a cultural naming tradition?

6. What is the quality/nature of human relationships within families in the culture?

7. What are your family's attitudes toward sex and sexuality? the culture's?

8. What are your family's attitudes toward marriage and family? the culture's?

9. What occupations or types of work are represented by your ancestors? Are these choices typical of the culture?

10. What are your family's attitudes toward work and vocation? the culture's?

11. What are your family's attitudes toward education? the culture's?

12. What place does religion play in your family? in the culture?

13. What is the culture's attitude toward material versus spiritual values?

14. What are the most difficult intergenerational issues of families in this culture?

15. What difficulties did members of this culture have in adjusting to mainstream society? What was different for the first versus the second generation (or, if relevant, for the third, fourth, or fifth generations) in the United States?

16. What are the culture's greatest strengths for coping/adjusting?

17. How are conflicts/disagreements resolved in your family? in the culture?

18. What other cultural groups are (were) most respected? For what reason(s)?

19. What other cultural groups are (were) least respected? For what reason(s)?

20. Is the traditional culture still intact or has it changed greatly? Is there still a cultural community (i.e., Chinatown, Little Italy, etc.)?

21. What historical dates, beliefs, attitudes are (were) most important to this culture?

22. Were biracial, biethnic, or bireligious marriages common? How were such relationships perceived, encouraged, and/or discouraged within the culture?

23. Multiculturally speaking, what does your interviewee think are the major problems in cross-cultural issues today? Does she or he believe this common viewpoint would be held by others of the same cultural heritage?

24. As a last part of the interview, you might ask the interviewee to identify:

    a. His or her most common gripes about life, society, etc.

    b. What most needs to be done in society to improve it.

After the interview, you might reflect on what continuous patterns of behavior, beliefs, attitudes, and so on still seem to exist within the cultural group or are evident in your own living patterns/lifestyle.

1. Are you "living up to" your family of origin's expectations? How or how not?

2. Are you "living up to" your family's culture's expectations? How or how not?

3. If there are differences, how do you cope with these?

   With family differences:

   With culture differences:

4. What do you think a person of another culture (pick one) would think of your culture as you have "discovered" it?

5. Share your conclusions with those interviewed for their reactions. Show them to a nonfamily member of your culture to see if his/her reactions approximate yours.

6. What of importance did you discover in this exercise?

   About self?

   About family?

   About culture?

   About others?

NOTE: In Section III of this manual, "Heightening Our Awareness and Knowledge of Others," you are also encouraged to interview persons of a different cultural background. A similar questionnaire is used for this purpose and will assist you to make comparisons to your own culture.

ACTIVITY II-6
Thinking about Your Family Heritage

In addition to the questions researched in the family member cultural interview, respond to the following questions:

1. What does your surname mean? Be sure to consider both your mother's and your father's surnames. Has your surname ever been changed? When? Why?

2. What does your first name mean? Is there an expectation of you associated with this name? How was it chosen? Does it "sound" like a name in your cultural group?

3. What is the meaning of other family members' first names (mother, father, siblings, grandparents, aunts, uncles, cousins)?

4. Are there traditional names passed from generation to generation?

5. How are previous generations remembered? What stories have come down to you about grandparents, great-grandparents, and so on?

6. How did your parents meet? Your grandparents meet? Is there a cultural ritual/pattern to courtship and marriage?

7. Are there favorite sayings or superstitions in your family? Is there an explanation for them?

8. What discoveries about your heritage stand out the most for you?

9. Imagine that you are 103 years old and want to pass on this heritage to a young child. Write an essay that would accurately express this heritage.

ACTIVITY II-7
Cultural Impacts upon Counseling

Cultural Conditioning

When human services counselors listen carefully to the words that they or other professional colleagues are saying, the words often reveal the point they have reached in their personal/professional development. A basic first step for you to take is to assess whether expressed attitudes, feelings, or behaviors might be potentially negative or potentially positive for effective functioning in a cross-cultural relationship. The following are examples of conversations gathered from human relations and cross-cultural workshops as well as public conversations that demonstrate both negative and positive cultural conditioning.

Negative Conditioning

1. "As a community worker and Anglo American, I sense a lack of confidence in myself toward certain medical doctors in my health clinic. These doctors are usually dark skinned, with black hair, speak with a Spanish accent, and usually have

a Spanish surname or foreign-sounding name. Sometimes I discover that their background is Puerto Rican, Filipino, or South-Asian Indian."

2. "As an African American and social worker, I have known for a long time that most Whites are very ignorant of the personal and historical problems of Blacks in America. I find myself feeling very impatient and intolerant of such ignorance in my professional associates as well as in my clients. Basically, I have little respect for these kinds of people and avoid being around them or having anything personally to do with them."

3. "Every time I hear a woman talking about discrimination against women by men, I figure the odds are she must be a lesbian who hates men."

Positive Conditioning

1. "I have a colleague at my agency who, when his progress with minority clients seems to slow down or go astray, often makes comments like, 'There's no end to these people,' or 'It's always the ones with the low income and education who breed the most.' It makes me feel very uncomfortable when I hear this because I realize it's a put-down as well as using the client's situation as an excuse. I'd like to confront this, but I'm not sure how to go about it without offending the person."

2. "I never really met Chicano people, or Latinos, or Spanish-speaking people. I grew up in a rural area in almost total isolation from different people. That is, until I took this job as school counselor. I can honestly say that I don't really understand why they always want to know about my personal life, and I wonder why they give me blank stares when I ask them to tell me something about themselves so I can get to know them. I want to be effective with all my clients, and I'm beginning to realize I have a lot to learn."

3. "I've noticed that Blacks in our country don't get recognition for positive things they accomplish and the things they really believe in."

4. "It really makes me feel worthwhile to hear my elderly retired clients open up when I conduct my 'Friends to Friends' workshop. I really believe there's a lot of prejudice and resentment toward older people. I find they have wonderful ideas and interesting experiences to relate."

Identifying, Exploring, and Modifying or Strengthening Cultural Conditioning

Honest expressions of both negative and positive conditioning can be taken as a starting point for structured change and improvement. People who express *negative* conditioning should not be viewed as hopeless cases, rather their development should be accepted for what it is and what it could be. People who express a level *of positive* conditioning can be assisted toward even higher levels of effective functioning.

The following worksheets are best used with small groups of participants (two to four), preferably of different genders and ethnic backgrounds where possible. The first step is for each person to identify at least two personal aspects that he or she can honestly admit might be personal examples of negative conditioning. For some participants this is very difficult, whereas for others it is very readily accomplished. Often, closing one's eyes and centering on one's own inner self for a few minutes can facilitate the identification stage. Sharing the identified aspects is the next step, followed by exploring, and finally discovering how the identified aspects might be *modified*. For positive conditioning, the same procedure of identifying, exploring, but then *strengthening* is followed. Group assistance, trust, and respect are essential qualities necessary to promote the open expression of thoughts and feelings that people fear others would reject them for having. Members of the group should recognize that each member will need the assistance of the others to clarify (identify), discover (explore), and change (modify or strengthen) attitudes, feelings, or behaviors that have been self-identified by each group member. An open, nonthreatening process of sharing one's perceptions of another's answers will encourage this process.

A. Negative Cultural Conditioning

IDENTIFYING

Attitudes, feelings, or behaviors that I believe are personally nongrowth-producing for me as a self-confident person and that hinder, or could hinder, my effectiveness and success as a professional worker. Examples are:

1.

2.

EXPLORING

What are my personal motives?

1. What will I gain by supporting this conditioning?

2. How am I benefiting from this conditioning?

3. What price am I paying for maintaining this conditioning?

4. What is my worst fantasy of what could happen if I modify this conditioning?

MODIFYING

What specific action plans can I take to modify or weaken this conditioning?

1. Is this action feasible? Am I capable of carrying it out?

2. What resources do I have to help me?

3. How realistic is this plan in my situation?

B. Positive Cultural Conditioning

IDENTIFYING

Attitudes, feelings, or behaviors that I believe are personally growth-producing for me as a self-confident person and that further, or could further, my effectiveness and success as a professional worker. Examples are:

1.

2.

EXPLORING

What are my personal motives?

1. What will I gain by supporting this conditioning?

2. What will I lose by supporting this conditioning?

3. What needs of my own would I satisfy if I strengthened this conditioning?

STRENGTHENING

What specific action can I take to support or strengthen this conditioning?

1. Is the action feasible? Am I capable of accomplishing it?

2. What resources do I have to help me?

3. How realistic is this plan in my situation?

SUMMARY OF SECTION II
Cultural Self-Awareness

Now take the time to reflect on the information discovered in the self-awareness activities. Identify the most critical ideas relevant to:

1. Your self-identity.

2. Your cross-cultural relationships.

3. Expanding your contacts with different others.

4. Increasing your multicultural knowledge.

5. List those ideas about which you should be critically cautious (e.g., avoiding assumptions).

6. Based on your work in Section II, what message, idea, or perception about multiculturalism would you like to share with yourself or your colleagues at this time?

7. Now list any newly discovered sources from which you could obtain information of a multicultural nature.

SOURCE (book, film, etc.)	NATURE/TYPE OF SOURCE	WHERE TO FIND IT (address, phone, etc.)
1.		
2.		
3.		
4.		
5.		
6.		
7.		
8.		

III

Heightening Our Awareness and Knowledge of Others

Background Reading: Chapter 3, "Profiles of the American People: Native Americans, Anglo-Americans, European Ethnic Americans" and Chapter 4, "Profiles of the American People: African Americans, Hispanic Americans, Asian Americans," in John A. Axelson, *Counseling and Development in a Multicultural Society* (3rd ed.). Pacific Grove, Calif.: Brooks/Cole, 1999.

FOR YOUR CONSIDERATION

High levels of self-identity as related to a positive identification with one's heritage (cultural) group is often associated with high levels of mental health and self-esteem. While claiming one's cultural identity is encouraged, an often underemphasized issue for many is how to accept a biracial, biethnic, bicultural identity. It appears that many persons in the United States (as well as in other nations) tend to be pushed to claim one parent's heritage over the other parent's heritage. Think of the difficulties this presents to such a person as an individual, as a member of one rather than the other culture grouping, and as a member of the general society and world. For example, how would you react if someone identified him- or herself as a Black/White American or as a Japanese/Mexican American rather than African American or Japanese American? And now there are many "cross-heritage/transracial" adoptees. An individual might accept and be quite satisfied with his or her bicultural identity. However, in general, societal structure and norms still tend to pressure the individual to "declare" only one heritage and treat the person as either "this" or "that."

Today the United States of America is one of the most culturally pluralistic nations in the world. The heterogeneity of this land has been a documented historical fact for over 500 years regardless of the national government. Indeed, the Native American populations inhabiting the North American landmass have been heterogeneous since before recorded history. In the context of this past and current cultural diversity, the United States has been and is a rich laboratory for multicultural learning.

There are many ways in which we all have been exposed to "knowing about" the diverse peoples who have lived and worked in this nation in the past as well as currently. Our "education" about people of difference takes place within the context of our educational, career, and social experiences in societal institutions such as family, school, profession, and religion. The various media—newspapers, movies, books, art and architecture, theater, and song—have often depicted and defined our images of the many different cultures present in this society. Our families may have shared stories that encouraged certain perceptions and understandings of other cultures. We also have personal, individual, and group experiences at work, play, and school that influence our perceptions and understandings of "different others." All these experiences reaffirm our own sense of cultural identity as well as highlight differences from other peoples. We might recognize that we evaluate others not only in terms of what we know (and don't know) about their cultural heritage but also in terms of what we know (and don't know) about our own heritage. For example, a young child playing "cowboys and Indians" may be creating a personal definition about both non-Native and Native Americans, regardless of historical accuracy.

The focus in many of the following activities suggests that we examine differences between ourselves and others in terms of culture, and/or race, and/or ethnicity. However, we are also simultaneously members of any number of subcultural groupings or categories of status that may impact upon our understanding of self as well as others. Human diversity in gender, sexual orientation, religion, membership in particular social groups (e.g., gangs, professions, clubs, teams, etc.) or in groupings (the young, the elderly, homosexuals, the disabled) or in economic categories (rich, poor, middle class) often plays a major role in defining who we are, who others are, how others perceive us, how we perceive others, and how we relate to them and they to us. We encourage you to consider these elements of diversity as you examine cultural, racial, or ethnic-based issues of difference.

In the face of numerous information and learning experiences and a changing United States, we encourage you to increase your exposures to persons or groups different from yourself. We believe that our most useful understandings of others and self in relationship to others develop from such contacts. In the activities that follow, you may find that you cannot provide answers as some questions may not be pertinent to your life experience. Nevertheless, when appropriate and possible, make an effort to discover the information that you currently lack. Also, many of the activities can also be easily modified to explore other issues of human diversity. We encourage you to do so; for example, you might explore differences and/or similarities that seem to be based on religious beliefs, gender, age, and/or subcultural groupings.

ACTIVITY III-1
Assimilation versus Cultural Pluralism

The history of the settling of North America has always involved a relationship between the earliest immigrants and Native Americans as well as with the many groups of immigrants that followed. Today, as diverse cultural groups continue to migrate to the United States and as other groups such as those based on religion, sex, age, race, or sexual orientation express a desire for recognition, the melting pot concept has been challenged. The melting pot concept envisioned diverse cultures merging into a single United States culture while the currently popular concept of "cultural pluralism" emphasizes diversity within unity.

The following questionnaire offers statements that are representative of cultural assimilation or cultural pluralism. That is, they delineate attitudes that either favor mainstream, dominant culture or favor a pluralistic point of view. Absolute true or false responses to many of the statements are, of course, not possible, and different individuals will have different opinions. Go through the 17 statements and respond according to your own viewpoint.

STATEMENT	TRUE	FALSE	NOT SURE/ NO ANSWER
1. Individual hard work and perseverance are the only important qualities that will win big rewards in the United States.		X	
2. Immigrant groups that are similar to the original European settlers are most likely to accept their values and views by the time of the third generation.		X	
3. White male Protestants in the United States hold most of the top managerial and leadership positions and will probably continue to do so for a long time.	X		
4. Jewish Americans are educationally and economically successful out of proportion to their numbers in the country.		X	
5. Most ethnic groups are equally distributed throughout the social, political, and economic structure.		X	
6. Middle-class and lower-class socioeconomic groups in the United States do not disagree on what is desirable and what is undesirable for living a "quality" life.		X	
7. Membership in an ethnic group determines social status.		X	
8. Most, if not all, ethnic groups in the United States want to assimilate into mainstream cultural ways.		X	
9. Different ethnic and racial groups in the United States today continue to have different ideas about what is desirable for their groups.	X		

STATEMENT	TRUE	FALSE	NOT SURE/ NO ANSWER
10. An ethnic or racial group that holds on to its traditions and identity may have an advantage in the United States today.			X
11. The economic and social interests of an ethnic group in the United States today are more important than its culture, language, and religion as such.	X		
12. Eventually, it is the government or governmental policy that determines or decides who (or which group) gets the benefits of the system.		X	
13. People in the United States have or can attain equal opportunity when they accept the basic American way.	X		
14. People in the United States' majority culture are ranked in a system of social stratification that gives status.	X		
15. To get ahead in the United States today means to take advantage of the educational, economic, and political opportunities that are available.	X		
16. To get ahead in the United States today means to develop one's unique individual potential as a first priority.	X		
17. To get ahead in the United States today means to strengthen your ties with the group with which you most readily identify.		X	

Assimilation View

1. true
2. true
3. ?
4. true
5. false
6. true
7. false
8. true

Cultural Pluralism View

1. false.
2. ?
3. ?
4. true
5. false
6. true
7. true
8. false

Assimilation View	Cultural Pluralism View
9. true	9. true
10. false	10. true
11. true	11. false
12. true	12. true
13. true	13. false
14. false	14. true
15. true	15. true
16. true	16. false
17. false	17. true

A. What viewpoint do you tend to hold? *Cultural Pluralism View*

B. What viewpoint do you believe your cultural group might hold? *Assimilation*

C. What did you discover about yourself? About how others might have answered?

I discovered that I believe these groups/diff. groups should be able to live in the U.S. + have their own culture. Isn't that what the U.S. is all about?

ACTIVITY III-2
Comparing Cultural Values

1. Develop a list of 10 values that are important to your cultural/racial identity. List these in the left column under "Values" on the chart that follows. (You could refer back to the values listed in Activity I-3.)

Values	RANKINGS								
	Self 1	Self 2	Self 3	D/S 1	D/S 2	D/S 3	D/N 1	D/N 2	D/N 3
a.									
b.									
c.									
d.									
e.									
f.									
g.									
h.									
i.									
j.									

2. In the Self 1 (self-culture) column, rank these values from 1 to 10 (1 = most important; 10 = least important).

3. Ask two persons of your same cultural/ethnic/racial background (or similar grouping such as age, gender, etc.) to rank these same values, in columns Self 2 and Self 3. Do not show them your rankings until after their rankings are complete.

4. Ask three persons of a "different yet similar" culture or grouping also to rank order these same values in columns D/S 1, D/S 2, and D/S 3. Do not show them the previous rankings until they have completed theirs.

5. Ask three persons of a "different and *not* similar" culture or grouping also to rank these values in columns D/N 1, D/N 2, and D/N 3. Again, do not show them the previous rankings until they have completed theirs.

6. Are there ranking differences *within* any cultural group or groupings?

7. Is there any value ranked the same by all persons of all groups or groupings?

8. Compute the "average" ranking for each value for each group.

   a. Are there any negligible differences in ranking for any values among the groups (that is, list values for which there seems to be consensus among the three groups)?

   b. Are there any large differences in ranking for any values (that is, there seems to be little agreement among the three groups for what values)?

9. Did anyone (or group) seem to object to including any particular value listed on the chart? If so, which value(s)?

10. Did anyone (or group) suggest that there was a value not listed that absolutely should have been listed? If so, which value(s)?

11. Are the samples of responses too small to reliably suggest anything of a truly useful nature? What might the responses suggest if they were representative of an entire culture?

12. What is your reaction? Were there any surprises? What does this exercise suggest about the data (e.g., such as limited personal experiences) that we use as a basis for our understandings of cultures, races, or ethnic groups different from ourselves?

ACTIVITY III-3
Friendship Networks

1. Identify persons of a different culture, race, ethnicity, or other element of human diversity who you consider to be close friends.

   a. *Bridget*

   b. *Mark*

   c. *Mairead*

   d. *Mark*

   e.

2. How did you become close friends?

   College, when I was younger, work, family

3. Have there been difficult periods in the friendship? If so, describe them.

   Yes – brother-in-law – can't figure out why he does things – still trying to understand italian culture.

   Yes – friend → told me ~~during~~ college she was a lesbian not too difficult

4. How were these difficulties resolved?

   Trying to talk and understand

5. Did you discover any differences between how you approached such difficulties and the way you have usually approached difficulties within your family or with persons of your own cultural heritage? – *Yes more hesitant to say anything*

6. What significant understandings relative to resolving *differences with people who are different from you* did you develop? Which of these have been useful in forming/maintaining other close relationships?

   Learning about their differences and learning to love them for who they are

ACTIVITY III-4
Can You Remember?

1. At what age(s) over your life span have you had personal, direct contact with someone of a different culture/race/ethnicity? Begin with the earliest recollection and move forward to the present. What was the setting—home, school, and so on? What was the nature of the contact—dinner guest, classmate, playmate? Add any comments or impressions of these recollections. (Use extra paper if necessary.)

MY AGE	PERSON OF DIFFERENCE	SETTING	NATURE OF CONTACT	COMMENTS
4	- girl my mom babysat	my house	playmate	russian - after school
9	Ireland - Shauna Mairead	my house	Project children	stayed with us 6 weeks over the summer for 5 summers
12	Tawana Brown black	school	friend in school	didn't hang out outside of school
12	Mike Chico mixed	"	"	friend
12	Tiffany Linney	" mixed	friend school →	
12	Lara Kassel	school	friend	jewish
14				

(left margin: 5 → Derek Seward, Norman Caldwell elementary school)

2. Identify your earliest exposures to different others through movies or television shows, including newscasts. What was the story about? What were your reactions or impressions?

MY AGE	PERSON OF DIFFERENCE	MEDIA	NATURE OF STORY	REACTIONS
10	Cosby's	t.v.	family	liked it alot

3. Identify your earliest exposures to different others through newspapers, story books, novels, magazines. What was the story about? Who was the hero, the villain? What was your reaction?

MY AGE	PERSON OF DIFFERENCE	MEDIA	NATURE OF STORY	REACTIONS
12	Iggie's House	book		

4. Identify any other exposures to people of difference you might have had—for example, as neighbors, through religious observances, or sports events.

MY AGE	PERSON OF DIFFERENCE	SITUATION	REACTIONS

5. In thinking about such contacts, try to recall whether significant others—such as family, friends, teachers, religious leaders—were also present.

   a. How much influence did these significant others have over you?

   b. If they made comments, what was the nature of their comments?

   c. Did you argue, dispute, agree, or ignore the comments?

   d. Have your perceptions changed over time? If so, how did this change happen; that is, what prompted you to change your perception/understanding of others?

6. In reflecting on these experiences (particularly the earliest ones):

   a. Do you have any perceptions about others' differentnesses that have remained rather constant over your life span?

   b. Would you judge these perceptions of differentnesses to hold generally true about an entire group of persons as represented in your experience?

   c. Would you judge such perceptions as increasing or decreasing your ability to be nonjudgmental of others as well as understanding differentnesses?

7. Your perceptions or understanding of others are to some degree limited by the experiences you have had. Given this condition, how would you try to expand your understanding? Make a list of the things you could do to expand your awareness of different others. (Be specific; make a plan for a specific culture.)

ACTIVITY III-5
Learning to Be Sensitive: Making a Tally

1. How many persons of a different culture, race, or ethnicity, or others whom you think of as different, live near you?

a. In the same apartment building, next door, or nearby? How do you describe their differentness?

(1)

(2)

(3)

(4)

b. How many different cultures, races, ethnic groups, or others you think of as different live in the larger society or community (that is, throughout the metropolitan region)? How do you describe their differentness?

(1)

(2)

(3)

(4)

2. If you were asked to describe the above persons as different from you, how would you do so? Try to identify at least three aspects of differentness—for example, in physical appearance, cultural practices, beliefs, values, behaviors.

a. Person 1

b. Person 2

c. Person 3

d. Person 4

3. Do you have a friend who is a member of any of these groups? Could you comfortably share your list of differentness (in item 2 above) with her or him?

   a. What is his or her reaction?

   b. What is your reaction to that reaction?

   c. Would you now change anything on your list?

4. If you do not think you could comfortably share your list, why not? Explain your reasons.

5. Are you aware of any cultural associations, organizations, clubs, or events that your neighbors of difference belong to or participate in? List them and identify their purpose.

ORGANIZATION	PURPOSE

6. Have you ever participated in these organizations or events? Identify an organization or experience (e.g., Chinese New Year, NAACP, American Indian Center).

   a. What did you learn about the culture(s) by participating? (Perhaps you were surprised by something that occurred.)

b. How did members of the group react to you?

c. What did you learn about yourself or about your own culture?

d. What do you learn by not having participated? Are perceptions of others passively reinforced by not having such experiences?

ACTIVITY III-6
Discoveries through Travel

1. Have you ever visited the country of origin of an ethnic/cultural group different from your own? List them.

   a.

   b.

   c.

   d.

2. Have you ever visited the community of an ethnic/cultural group different from your own (e.g., a Little Italy, Chinatown)? List them.

   a.

   b.

   c.

   d.

3. Have you ever been in the home of a person of a different ethnic/cultural background? List the groups represented.

   a.

   b.

   c.

   d.

4. Did you notice any behaviors or beliefs exhibited in these travels that do (or do not) reflect a similarity to the behavior of a person (or the group) of this heritage living in the United States? (For example, how similar is the behavior of Greek Americans with native Greeks living in Greece?)

GROUP	SIMILARITY	DISSIMILARITY

5. Have you discovered any behaviors, beliefs, or values of North Americans (specifically, the United States) that can most likely be traced to their country of origin? List them.

   a.

   b.

   c.

   d.

6. Are such culturally based behaviors as useful in the United States as they might be in the place of origin?

   a. How so?

   b. How not so?

   c. How difficult might it be to change a behavior that may have been reinforced for many generations both in the United States as well as in the original homeland?

      (1) What *intrapersonal* difficulties might one experience if that person chose to change a culturally reinforced and expected behavior?

(2) What *interpersonal* difficulties might one experience if that person chose to change a culturally reinforced and expected behavior:

(a) Within their family?

(b) Within their culture as a whole?

(c) With other cultures in the society?

7. You may have perceived a culturally based behavior that was directed at you as an effort to offend you personally. Can you identify any culturally based behaviors that are different from your own culturally learned ways of relating to others? List them. (Consider ways of saying hello, doing business transactions, expressing opinions, performing rituals, using eye contact, etc.)

a.

b.

c.

d.

ACTIVITY III-7
Interviewing Different Cultures

In order to explore other cultures further, we suggest you now identify and interview at least four persons of a culture different from your own. You might choose one different culture from your earlier work (Section I) in which you identified a group that was "different yet similar" to your own. We suggest that the second, third, and fourth different interviews be chosen from the "different and not similar" groups. Consider also a different format; for example, interviewing two persons from within each of two "different cultures," or choosing one who is elderly and one who is young, or one female and one male.

Your own creative thinking can generate any number of variables for this activity. However, it is important to remember that such variables may introduce issues of unique, individual experience that may or may not be indicative of the culture as a whole. Also, recall that shared information specific to incidents within a family cannot necessarily be generalized to the whole group. Try to distinguish between such specific family history and what is common throughout the culture.

Use the following questions in your interviews. Review the questions and create others you think should be asked. In a previous essay (Activity I-6) you wrote about "What It Is Like to Be a Person of a Different Culture." One of your interviewees should be a person from the group about whom you wrote your essay.

Cross-Cultural Interview Questions

1. What is the average size and composition of the family in this culture?

2. What is the authority structure of the family in this culture?

3. What are the role concepts within the family system in this culture?

4. How would the interviewee describe the emotional/psychological "personality" of his or her family—that is, aggressive, reserved, outgoing, etc.?

5. Does the interviewee believe his or her family is similar or dissimilar to most other families within their culture? If dissimilar, how so?

6. What is the nature of male/female relationships within the culture?

7. What are the cultural attitudes toward sex and sexuality?

8. What are the cultural attitudes toward marriage and family life?

9. What are the cultural attitudes toward work and vocation? Is there a historical or present-time pattern of certain kinds of jobs or careers held or pursued by this culture?

10. What are the cultural attitudes toward education?

11. What place does religion play in this culture?

12. What is the cultural attitude toward material versus spiritual values?

13. What are the most difficult intergenerational issues of families in this culture?

14. What is the nature of difficulties in adjusting to the United States society? What was different for the first versus second generation (or third, fourth, and fifth generations) in the United States?

15. What are the cultural strengths for coping/adjusting? In the past? In the present?

16. How are conflicts/disagreements resolved between members of this culture?

17. What other cultures are most respected by this culture? For what reason(s)?

18. What other cultural groups were most respected? For what reason(s)?

19. What other cultural groups are least respected? For what reason(s)?

20. What historical periods, beliefs, attitudes, and values are most important to this culture?

21. Can the interviewee identify whether his or her own ways of thinking and behaving are similar to parents', grandparents', and neighbors' ways of thinking and behaving? Ask for examples.

22. Were biracial, biethnic, or bireligious marriages common? How were such relationships encouraged or discouraged within the culture?

23. Is there another culture that members of this culture *always* have difficulty with? What is the nature of the difficulty?

24. Is there a culture that members of this culture rarely have difficulty with? What is the reason for the lack of difficulty?

25. Are there certain ways that this cultural group is generally discriminated against by other cultural groups in the United States? How is this done and has your interviewee, as an individual, had such an experience?

26. Multiculturally speaking, what does your interviewee think are the major problems in cross-cultural relations today? Is this a common viewpoint by others of the same cultural heritage?

As when interviewing members of your own culture, be aware that cross-cultural interviewees' answers may not always accurately represent attitudes that are culturally widespread and representative of the whole culture. However, you may discover a recurring transgenerational pattern of beliefs, attitudes, and behaviors.

As in the earlier self-culture interview, you might also ask the interviewees:

1. Are you "living up to" your family of origin's expectations? How or how not?

2. Are you "living up to" your culture's expectations? How or how not?

3. If there are differences, how do you cope with these?

    a. With your family of origin?

    b. With your culture?

4. What of importance did you (the interviewer) discover in this exercise?

    a. About self:

    b. About family:

    c. About others:

5. As a last part of the interview, you might ask the interviewees to identify:

   a. Their most common gripes about life, society, and so on.

   b. What most needs to be done in society to improve it.

After the interviews, reflect on the similarities and dissimilarities between your own culture and these different cultures. Compare each of your interview answers to theirs. In general:

1. Were there any surprises? What are they?

2. How would you account for any differences discovered; that is, what might have caused these differences to develop?

3. How would you account for any similarities discovered; that is, what might have caused these similarities?

4. If your "What It Is Like to Be a Person of a Different Cultural Heritage" essay (Activity I-6) was about the cultures represented in your interviews:

   a. Would you now say something different? What?

   b. How generally accurate or inaccurate was your essay?

   c. Would you share your essay with the interviewee? Explain why or why not.

5. Summarize what you have discovered in these cross-cultural exchanges:

   a. About self:

   b. About family:

   c. About culture in general:

   d. About others' cultures:

   e. About your own culture:

ACTIVITY III-8
Cultural Profiles

Given all your sources of information (your interviews, experiences, background readings, movies, newspapers), develop a cultural profile for each of the following groups (see the form on pages 78–79; make additional copies as necessary). This profile may be developed by yourself or with a group of friends.

1. Native Americans

2. Anglo-Saxon Americans

3. White Ethnic Americans

4. Black Americans

5. Hispanic Americans

6. Asian Americans

After you have completed the six profiles, follow these steps:

1. Call or visit with a staff person of a community organization such as a cultural association or human services agency that serves each culture. Share your cultural profile with them. (Several agencies and associations are listed in Appendix A; similar organizations can be found in other cities or areas.)

2. How accurate were you? List below the:

   a. Items clarified or expanded upon:

   b. Items disputed or corrected:

   c. New items to be added:

   d. Items to be deleted:

3. Modify your cultural profile accordingly.

4. Summarize what you have learned from this experience in the summary statement on the "Culture Heritage Group in Profile" form that follows.

CULTURE HERITAGE GROUP IN PROFILE   Culture: _____

The following information represents your understanding of this cultural group according to your cultural interview as well as perceptions based on knowledge from other sources of information.

Group primary descriptors (national origins, physical and behavioral characteristics, etc.):

Group secondary descriptors (list characteristics of this group; include information that addresses each of the following):

Values/beliefs:

Perceptions of the world:

Methods of settling conflict:

Methods of ensuring conformity:

Group personality:

Relationship to other groups:

What is most important to achieve (in lifetime):

Unique behaviors and what they mean:

Historical events of critical importance to this cultural group:

CULTURE HERITAGE GROUP IN PROFILE *(continued)*

Other critical information relevant to understanding this culture:

1.

2.

3.

4.

5.

6.

What is similar or dissimilar to your own cultural heritage?
Similar   *Dissimilar*

List key ideas and behaviors that would increase the likelihood of being able to relate well to this culture:

Summary statement regarding this culture:

ACTIVITY III-9
Activities to Discover Human Diversity

Appendix A contains a list of ethnic museums and agencies and associations compiled for your review (there are similar resources in most cities and areas). There are also listings of books, movies, and plays that also explore some of the vast range of cultural and subcultural issues in society. We encourage you to select several items from this list for your enjoyment and further learning. Identify your selections below and summarize what you have discovered.

ACTIVITY	SUMMARY
1.	
2.	
3.	

SUMMARY OF SECTION III
Heightening Our Awareness and Knowledge of Others

At this point, reflect on the information discovered in the activities for Section III, "Heightening Our Awareness and Knowledge of Others." Identify the most critical ideas relevant to:

1. Your self-identity.

2. Your cross-cultural relationships.

3. Expanding your contacts with different others.

4. Suggestions for increasing your multicultural knowledge.

5. List ideas about which you should be critically cautious.

6. Based on your work in Section III, what message, idea, or perception about multi-culturalism would you like to share with yourself or your colleagues at this time?

7. List any newly discovered sources from which you obtained information of a multicultural nature.

SOURCE (book, film, etc.)	NATURE/TYPE OF SOURCE	WHERE TO FIND IT (address, phone, etc.)
1.		
2.		
3.		
4.		
5.		
6.		
7.		
8.		

SECTION

IV

Awareness and Knowledge of Sociopolitical Issues

Background Reading: Chapter 5, "Social Political Issues," in John A. Axelson, *Counseling and Development in a Multicultural Society* (3rd ed.). Pacific Grove, Calif.: Brooks/Cole, 1999.

FOR YOUR CONSIDERATION

Is labeling only the nationals of the North American continent "Americans" accurate? Is labeling citizens of the United States "Americans" (while those of Canada are Canadians and those of Mexico are Mexicans) accurate? What should citizens who reside in South American countries be called? One's identity is also a product of national and international sociopolitical views and relationships. In most parts of the world a citizen of the United States is called "an American." What does this mean to you? What is an American? Do you (or others) distinguish between an identity associated with heritage (for example, Japanese American, Iranian American, etc.) versus national origin (Japanese or American or Jamaican or Russian or Colombian, etc.).

There are many physical, cognitive, affective, and behavioral characteristics that uniquely distinguish us from all other individuals. However, many of these uniquenesses are similar to characteristics commonly found among members of our own racial or ethnic group. Such characteristics common to members of one group often distinguish this group from other groups. For example, Patrick, Daniel, and Ralph McGrath (Irish-heritage siblings) are individually unique; yet, as members of a particular White/ethnic grouping, the McGraths are easy to identify as overtly different from Idi, Nora, and Christian Akiwowo (Black-Nigerian heritage). Such overt differences may be of major or minor importance both within as well as between groups. We must, however, also recognize that culturally reinforced ways of behaving, thinking, and feeling (about self, others, and the world) may have a powerful impact on our ability to understand and relate to a different cultural group. In other words, it is not so much that Patrick and Christian are White or Black, Irish or Nigerian, but rather what each thinks of Whites or Blacks, of Irish or Nigerians; how each behaves toward Whites or Blacks or Nigerians or Irish; how each feels about Whites or Blacks or Irish or Nigerians. And such ways of thinking, feeling, and behaving are

82

shaped and reinforced (approved of or disapproved of) by other members of their cultures, by other cultures, by the general society, and by nationals of other societies around the world.

Our identity, our ways of thinking, feeling, and behaving are commonly developed within the context of belonging to a specific group as well as one's family. Identity and behavior also develop in regard to how our own group interacts with and is perceived by other groups in the society at large and by nationals of other countries. How our own group is sociopolitically and socioeconomically positioned in the society is also of great importance. We are all members of a larger society (the United States) that has had (and appears to continue to have) a dominant "superculture" that has an all-pervasive influence upon all members and groups within this society as well as around the world. The differential experience of each individual or group is based in part on adherence to defined "ways of relating to others" as encouraged within the individual's own group and as practiced in interactions between groups. Further, these interactions occur in the context of the larger society's dominant themes. Sociopolitical concepts and practices, such as racism, ageism, sexism, bias, stereotyping, prejudice, and discrimination develop in the context of group reinforcement of how members should think, behave, and feel toward others.

While not always intentional and although people are not always aware of them, such understandings and practices often originate in the family and primary cultural group experiences.

We and the group to which we belong relate to and live in greater or lesser accord with dominant superculture themes. Whether our own particular racial/ethnic cultural group is more or less powerfully positioned in relationship to the total society (and to all other cultural groups as a whole) is of great importance.

Lastly, as noted previously, a host of other related sociopolitical role and status issues such as economic class, political affiliation or "leaning," gender and sexual orientation, religious belief, family role, job or career classification, age, health, and physical status also influence our behavior toward others and their behavior toward us. Membership in any such categories or combination thereof may mitigate or aggravate how an individual or group may be treated within one's culture group as well as by other cultures.

ACTIVITY IV-1
Getting in Touch with Your Own Social Identity

Social Roles

We communicate through our social roles. The roles we are known by (or make known to others) are often associated with certain self- and other-generated expectations of us. These roles often prompt a display of certain learned behaviors and beliefs by ourselves as well as by others.

Some aspects of our roles can be delineated according to:

1. Our socioeconomic, political, and religious characteristics, which imply a collection of perceived rights, duties, and expectations.

2. Our racial/ethnic, cultural/subcultural group membership, which may prompt differential treatment by others as well as influence our behavior toward them.

3. Our family roles, gender, age, and even living arrangements, which are associated with certain stereotypic expectations.

4. Our occupational status and level of education, which may also suggest we are supposed to be a certain kind of person.

The descriptors that may be used to identify oneself socially are varied and numerous. Many connote a powerful idea of the nature of person we are and the kind of behavior someone might expect of us. Such descriptors provide an "identity tag." We and others may use such labels to differentiate ourselves from others, compare ourselves to others, and even group ourselves with others. These labels encourage or define how we and others will interact with each other.

Some of our descriptors are ascribed, such as may occur by genealogy, chromosomes, or timing (e.g., Chinese, female, third generation). Many descriptors are also developed (e.g., we become conservative, we choose to be a mother, or we go to college). Some are chosen by self or others for their qualifying properties (e.g., "I'm African American not Black"). Of course, we all tend to believe that such descriptors, ascribed or achieved, do not automatically mean that our life and living is rigidly predefined or predetermined accordingly. Yet such conditions or statuses do influence us and others; oftentimes their negativity or positivity are of such significance that it is quite difficult to overcome or resist such a facet of self.

Identifying Selected Social Descriptors

1. In each of the four columns on page 85, check all the items that best describe you. Fill in blanks as you deem appropriate. Add data/information if needed. Some items may appear to overlap or could as easily be listed in a different column. Do not concern yourself with this fact.

2. Now circle the two or three items in each column that you deem *most important* in socially describing yourself to others at this point in your life.

3. According to my two or three circled items, the most important social descriptors at this time in my life are:

Column A: _____ _____ _____

Column B: _____ _____ _____

Column C: _____ _____ _____

Column D: _____ _____ _____

A: SOCIOPOLITICAL	B: RACIAL/ETHNIC	C: FAMILY/GENDER	D: OCCUPATION
Self-income, class	___ Afro-American	X Female	___ Business owner
___ low	___ African	Male	___ White-collar
X mid	American	X Married	___ Full professional
___ high	___ Black	___ Single	X Mid-level
Parents' income	___ Negro	___ Separated	professional
___ low	___ _____ American	Divorced	___ Entry-level
X mid	___ other _____	X Wife	professional
___ high		Husband	___ Technician
Generation in	___ Anglo-Saxon	___ Mother	___ Blue-collar worker
America	X White	___ Father	___ Skilled
___ 1st	___ _____ American	___ Stepparent	___ Clerk/office help
___ 2nd	___ White ethnic	___ Stepchild	___ Craftsman
___ 3rd	___ _____ American	Grandparent	___ Service provider
X 4th	___ other _____	X Aunt/uncle	___ Farmer
Political orientation	___ Native American	X Nephew/niece	___ other _____
___ radical	___ American Indian	X Daughter/son	___ Employer
___ liberal	___ _____ American	X Sister/brother	___ Employee
___ moderate	___ Inuit	___ Adoptive/foster	___ Supervisor
___ conservative	___ other _____	parent	___ Supervisee
X indifferent	___ Hispanic	___ Adopted/foster	___ Seniority
___ Republican	___ Latino	child	___ Type/field of work
___ Democrat	___ Chicano	___ Caretaker	
___ Independent	___ _____ American	___ Disciplinarian	X FT/PT worker
___ other	___ other _____	___ Homemaker	Education
Religious affiliation	___ Asian American	___ Breadwinner	X student
___ Protestant	___ Oriental	X Godparent	___ high school
X Catholic	American	_____ Age	___ college
___ Jewish (religion)	___ _____ American	_____ Type of	___ other _Grad_
___ Islamic	___ other _____	housing	X FT/PT student
___ Rastafarian	___ other _____	_____ # in	_____ age
___ Buddhist	___ other _____	household	___ Disabled
___ Hindu	___ other _____	Place of residence	___ other _____
___ N. Amer. Indian	___ Middle Eastern	___ urban	___ other _____
Church	American	X suburban	___ other _____
___ other _____	___ Semitic	___ rural	___ other _____
___ atheist/agnostic	American	___ other _____	
Other issues	___ _____ American	___ other _____	
_____	Other forms of	___ other _____	
_____	identifying self	___ other _____	
_____	_____		
_____	or ___-___		

4. With the above descriptions in mind, consider brief answers to the following questions.

   a. What are the advantages and disadvantages of being this kind of person in my personal life today? In my working life?

   Advantages   *Disadvantages*

   _____   _____

   _____   _____

   _____   _____

   b. What would be the advantages and disadvantages of being this kind of person in a minority community? (To answer this question, choose any minority group from column B, excluding your own.)

   Advantages   *Disadvantages*

   _____   _____

   _____   _____

   _____   _____

   c. What would be the advantages and disadvantages of being this kind of person in the majority community (i.e., the superculture of the United States)?

   Advantages   *Disadvantages*

   _____   _____

   _____   _____

   _____   _____

5. Given your descriptors of self and their advantages and disadvantages, what can you say about expectations we (and others) may have about others, based on such descriptors? Are they useful? In what ways? Do they influence us or others? How?

ACTIVITY IV-2
Influences of Social Identity

1. In Activity IV-1 you identified several characteristics that describe you. You further identified the advantages or disadvantages of being such a person. Now assign your characteristics to one or more of the subgroups listed under each of the following heritage groups. *Skip your own identity group.* (You can also identify some other subgroup of a particular heritage group that exists in your local community.) Then complete items 2, 3, and 4 following.

a. Native American:
   (1) Living on a reservation.
   (2) Living in a major metropolitan community.

b. Anglo-Saxon American:
   (1) From the New England region.
   (2) From Appalachia.
   (3) Amish from Pennsylvania.

c. White ethnic American (identify particular group):
   (1) Polish
   (2) Hungarian
   (3) Italian

d. African American:
   (1) From a southern or northern state.
   (2) Recent immigrant from Africa.
   (3) Living in a housing project.

e. Hispanic American:
   (1) Bolivian
   (2) Mexican
   (3) Puerto Rican

f. Asian American:
   (1) Vietnamese
   (2) Indian or Pakistani
   (3) Korean

2. Based on assigning your characteristics to persons of one or more of the above groups, answer the following questions for each group (or subgroup).

   a. What advantage or disadvantage would these characteristics be for this person in relation to the dominant U.S. culture?

   Advantages   *Disadvantages*

   _____   _____

   _____   _____

   _____   _____

   b. What advantage or disadvantage would these characteristics be for this person in relation to his or her own racial/ethnic cultural group?

   Advantages   *Disadvantages*

   _____   _____

   _____   _____

   _____   _____

c. In spite of any difficulties identified above, do you think the best course of action for all U.S. Americans is to move toward behavior that is in accord with dominant societal themes? Or should we move toward behavior that is in accord with our specific cultural heritage? Give reasons for your choice.

d. If choosing to remain true to their cultural heritage, which of the above groups might have the most difficulty contending with the dominant mainstream cultural themes? Why?

3. Is there an equally good fit of your most important characteristics with both your own culture and the other cultural groups?

a. Which other cultures fit?

How so? Explain.

b. Which other cultures don't fit?

How so? Explain.

4. Based on what you know of the values, beliefs, and practices of the different cultural groups identified above, what problems would a member of each group have *if she or he possessed your characteristics, but wanted to really fit in well in her or his own group?*

a. Would cultural role expectations create problems?

b. What advice would you give to this person as to how she or he might reconcile any role expectation conflicts with her or his own culture?

c. If this person seems to fit into both the dominant mainstream and the culture, would he or she still have difficulties? If so, what might they be?

d. What kind of difficulties might you have in regard to giving advice to this person?

Activity IV-3
Imagine that Your Social Identity Changed

In Activities IV-1 and 2, you based your answers upon selected social characteristics. Can you imagine what your answers would be if your characteristics changed? Can you imagine how your answers would change in regard to any of the persons listed in Activity IV-2? For example, reconsider what your answers would be if you (or the persons in the other groups) had:

1. A different income.

2. A different political orientation.

3. A different religious affiliation.

4. A different racial/ethnic cultural group.

5. A different gender.

6. A different sexual orientation.

7. A different family role/position.

8. A different age (plus or minus 15 years from your current age).

9. A different career/job classification.

In light of the "new" social characteristics you may have assigned to yourself (or another), what might be particularly different in your (or the other's) life? For example, would career opportunities be more or less limited? Would social acceptance within the general society be heightened or lessened? Based on this activity, list any new awareness that you think would improve your ability to understand persons who are "different" from you.

1.

2.

3.

Activity IV-4
Challenging Your Thoughts

1. Take any of your thoughts and ideas from the activities above and share them with another person of your heritage.

   a. Was your response supported by this person? In what way?

b. Was your response disputed by this person? In what way?

c. Do you now wish to rewrite any response? If so, identify it (or them) and explain your reasons for doing so.

2. Take any of your thoughts and ideas from the activities above and share them with a person or persons from one of the different heritages.

   a. Was your response supported by this person? In what way?

   b. Was your response disputed by this person? In what way?

   c. Do you now wish to rewrite any response? If so, identify it (or them) and explain your reasons for doing so.

3. Describe your experience in having your thoughts/ideas supported or disputed. How did it affect:

   a. Your thoughts?

   b. Your feelings?

   c. Your behaviors?

4. How might this experience affect you when relating to others in the future?

ACTIVITY IV-5
Can You Recognize Cultural Bias?

Bias is an inclination of our feelings or outlook. It is highly personal, and while it may not be meant intentionally to harm others, it often indicates a distortion in our judgment and/or awareness. Recognizing bias is an important step in developing awareness. We often exhibit bias in our speaking and writing without realizing it. Can you recognize bias in the following statements?

1. Although I knew he was an epileptic when I hired him, I was shocked when he had a fit in my office.

2. The ladies in our department outperform the men.

3. The company hired a person who was wheelchair bound.

4. She said one of the girls in the office must have typed the information and sent it to the order department.

5. The agency received a telephone call from an unemployed, African American construction worker who said his electricity had been turned off because his payment was not received.

6. If you remember, this applicant was that old lady.

ANSWERS:

1. Illness: Substitute "a person who has epilepsy" for "an epileptic." Substitute "seizure" for "fit."
2. Sex: Be consistent; use "women" and "men."
3. Illness: Substitute "uses a wheelchair" for "was wheelchair bound."
4. Sex: Use "secretaries" for "girls."
5. Race and job status: Both are irrelevant in this instance.
6. Age: Irrelevant reference to applicant; use "the woman."

Exchange nonbiased sentences for the following biased sentences.

1. The labor force needs skilled men.

2. Welcome, ladies and men.

3. Ask the girls to type the report.

4. Epileptics are dependable workers.

5. Sue is a Black friend of mine.

6. This is Mrs. John Brown.

ACTIVITY IV-6
Biting Your Own Tongue

Reflect on your answers to and discussions of the activities in this section. Be aware that a bias may indicate a favorable as well as unfavorable view of people, places, or things.

1. Do any of your responses reflect a bias? Identify them.

2. Did anyone (when sharing your responses) point out what appears to be a bias you have? What was it? Is there a theme to your bias?

3. Do you have a bias that you are particularly aware of? If you would like to change it, identify a plan for how you might attempt to modify this inclination to view people, places, or things in a distorted manner.

4. If you have a bias that might be considered favorable of another person or group, are there any negative implications to having it? What could be negative about a "favorable" bias?

ACTIVITY IV-7
Prejudice: A Circular Trap

> **INFORMATION:**
>
> The U.S. Equal Employment Opportunity Commission reported 70,339 complaints of job-related discrimination in 1992, the second highest annual total since the 1964 Civil Rights Act became law. Complaints of discrimination usually average around 60,000 per year. In 1992, 774 (1.1%) of the complaints were based on the new 1992 Americans with Disabilities Act. Discrimination based on race is the most frequently cited cause for complaints, accounting for 40.8% in 1992. Sex-based charges, mainly sexual harassment, accounted for 29.8% of all charges.

1. Prejudice is commonly associated with stereotyping behaviors and is often experienced when one is discriminated against. Prejudice is found throughout the world. Prejudice involves negative attitudes that are directed toward members of a group or toward an individual person. Prejudicial attitudes may also be directed toward places (such as geographic areas, communities, neighborhoods) or things (such as style of dress, customs, behaviors). The consequences of negative attitudes may be manifested in overt and covert discrimination or segregation.

   a. Are you aware of any prejudice displayed toward yourself?
      (1) Because of your race or ethnicity? No
      (2) Because of your sex? Yes
      (3) Because of some other characteristic of self? Young

   b. In the examples above, was the prejudice aimed at you as an individual or because you are a member of a particular grouping of people? Explain. Females young

   c. Are you aware of any prejudice you displayed toward others?
      (1) Because of their race or ethnicity? Yes
      (2) Because of their sex? No
      (3) Because of some other characteristic? Maybe

d. Talk to an older family member or friend and ask that person if he or she recalls any examples of prejudice (in the last 25 to 40 years) in your local community. *Yes ~ black family that moved in to neighborhood*

e. How might prejudice be used by people to actually increase their own self-esteem? *Making them feel like they belong to the majority*

2. Separating ourselves from strangers or people who are different from ourselves seems to be characteristic of human groups in general and can be noted in *social distancing.* The more different a group of people is from an individual, the more likely the individual is to stereotypically define them as less good, less important, less worthy, or even as inferior. Thus, the individual provides self-justification for treating them differently, unfairly, or perhaps even maliciously.

a. Identify ways you might have socially distanced yourself from others in the following situations. Explain your reasons.
(1) A room full of strangers
(2) A group of persons of a different race/ethnic group

b. Identify ways others have socially distanced themselves from you. What do you think the reasons were?
(1) Situation 1: *Elementary - all white*

(2) Situation 2:

c. Do you recall a time when another person stood too close (that is, when someone's physical closeness actually made you feel uncomfortable)?
No
(1) What did you do?
(2) What did you think regarding that person?
(3) Were there any cultural elements in this experience?
(4) If so, have they continued to influence you in other relationships with persons of this same culture?

d. Review what you have written above. Is there an element of justification for your behavior in any of these experiences? In the other person's behavior toward you?

3. People who are targets of stereotypes are often socialized to conform to the stereotypes. Stereotypic behavior by males and females is one example of incorporating learnings based on differential treatment beginning in infancy. Black persons, White ethnics, gays, and the elderly, among others, are potential victims of such learnings. The *self-fulfilling* phenomenon demonstrates that one's own behavior can bring about projected results. In this regard, unwarranted low self-esteem is often characteristic of target groups of prejudice.

a. List any examples of others telling you to conform to a certain way of behaving, thinking, or feeling that would be consistent with a particular stereotype. (For example, someone says to you, "You're Black [White, female, Irish, Chinese, a child, etc.] and you are should dress like . . .") Fill in the following blanks:

(1) You're a _____, so do _____.

(2) You're a _____, so don't _____.

(3) You're not a _____, so don't act like one.

b. How important is it to you for others to approve of you and your behavior? *Used to be very important*

c. Do you have a specific example of a time when you changed your behavior to conform to someone else's stereotype of how you should be? *Yes - highschool*

d. If you did not conform, how difficult was it not to and what were the consequences?

e. What did you do (would you do) the next time around? Why?

4. Individuals who show prejudice sometimes have authoritarian personalities; some others cannot vent frustrations against the proper sources so they *displace* their aggression onto a scapegoat. Still others have prejudice passed on by parents or others who act as models. Certain behaviors and attitudes may also be taught and reinforced by the media. Competition between groups and conformity to group norms can also encourage prejudice.

a. Has anyone ever "scapegoated" you? Identify some instances as in the following kinds of interactions with:
   (1) A sibling or parent.
   (2) Someone of a different race/ethnicity.
   (3) Someone of a higher economic level or different political belief.
   (4) Someone of a different sex. *Yes*
   (5) Someone of a different religious belief.
   (6) Someone of your peer group.

b. In any of the above instances, do you recall then displacing your anger toward someone "lower on the ladder"? Identify any instances below:

   (1)

   (2)

   (3)

   (4)

c. What was it about yourself (any characteristic you can think of) that made you the target of such scapegoating—that is, did you "invite" it to happen to you? *I was there*

d. What was it about another person (any characteristic you can think of) that made you target him or her as the scapegoat? Did that person "invite" it to happen to him or her?

e. Can you identify any instances of other people (or the media) scapegoating an individual because she or he was a member of a particular racial, ethnic, or other kind of grouping?

ACTIVITY IV-8
Assessing Experiences in Discrimination

Discrimination is often a systematized (organized) practice of prejudice that operates to "close the door" of equal opportunity or treatment. Discrimination may be intentional, or it may be unintentional due to an ignorance of what is fair to everyone (in contrast to what one *thinks* is fair to everyone). Discriminatory practice is generally aimed at all members of a particular grouping or category, not just a particular individual.

Complete the following questionnaire (page 96), and then answer questions 1–6. Write an explanation of all "yes" answers to questions 1–6, and share the explanations with another who is completing this activity. This should help you assess your understanding and experience of discrimination.

1. Have you ever been discriminated against because of:
   a. Your color?
   b. Your race/ethnicity?
   c. Your gender?
   d. Your age?
   e. Your religion?
   f. Your physical/health status?
   g. Your socioeconomic class?
   h. A subcultural group you identify with?

2. Has a family member ever been discriminated against because of:
   a. Color?
   b. Race/ethnicity?
   c. Gender?
   d. Age?
   e. Religion?
   f. Physical/health status?
   g. Socioeconomic class?
   h. A subcultural group the member identified with?

3. Do you have a friend who has been discriminated against because of:
   a. Color?
   b. Race/ethnicity?
   c. Gender?
   d. Age?
   e. Religion?
   f. Physical/health status?
   g. Socioeconomic class?
   h. A subcultural group the friend identified with?

4. What did you think about:
   a. The individual who actually did the discriminating?
   b. The racial/ethnic group of this individual?
   c. Others who may have "gone along" with the discrimination?

Discrimination Questionnaire (mark "yes" or "no" to all that apply; write an explanation for each yes answer)

1. Have you ever been stopped by the police because
   - of your cultural heritage?
   - of your skin color or other physical characteristics?
   - of the way you dress?
   - of your age?
   - you were in the "wrong" neighborhood? (at the wrong time?)
   - one of your passenger(s) was "different"?

2. Have you ever had an ancestor/family member who was hurt or died because of his/her heritage? Did this happen recently or a long time ago? How long ago?

3. Have you ever thought of not having children because of racism?

4. Have you ever thought you might not reach the age of 30?

5. Have you ever thought you did not get fair treatment in a job interview (or an "everyday" discussion)
   - for racial/cultural reasons?
   - for gender reasons?
   - for religious/belief reasons?

6. Have you ever "felt," "sensed" you were being "stared" at because you looked different from another person?

7. Have you ever been told/pressured by parents to stop "hanging out" with "so and so"?
   - told so by other adults (family members or acquaintances)?
   - told so by your friends?
   - told so by someone you didn't know but who "looked" like you?

8. Have you ever sat at a lunch/dinner and heard someone make disparaging comments about "them"?

9. Have you ever been glad you weren't or aren't treated like "so and so"?

10. Have you ever made a comment like "Well, if so and so just worked like me, they'd get ahead"?

11. Have you ever thought you "just need to treat others as people"?

12. Have you ever had a "loved relative"
    - who is blatantly racist or prejudiced?
    - who is subtly racist or prejudiced?
    - who you know discriminates against others?

13. Choose which of the following groups you would want to be reborn into. Choose any, but *not* your own heritage.
    African American
    Native American
    Hispanic American
    Asian American
    European American
    Arab American
    Jewish American
    Bi-racial American

14. Why did you make that choice for question 13 and not one of the other choices possible? Please explain or discuss with others who answer this questionnaire.

Partially adapted from: Lee Mun Wah, Director, Stir Fry Seminars, 470 Third St., Oakland, CA 94607. As presented in LaCrosse, Wisconsin, Racism Workshop, August 27, 1996.

5. How did you feel toward or behave toward:
   a. The individual who actually did the discriminating?
   b. The racial/ethnic group of this individual?
   c. The society as a whole?

6. If laws against discrimination do not fully work, what might be the best ways of combating such issues as racism, prejudice, discrimination, bias, and stereotyping of others? Identify some ideas (things you might do) that might be appropriate to try:
   a. As an individual.
   b. As a local community project.
   c. Nationwide.

ACTIVITY IV-8
Field Study and Observation

Research indicates that interpersonal contacts among group members characterized as cooperative and where members treat each other as equals result in less stereotypes, less social distancing, and a greater willingness to interact. Select a group (a class, campus, workplace, church, team) to observe and study. Look for characteristics of interdependency, cooperation, equal status with one another, informality, and shared goals. Can you estimate the level of prejudice and stereotyping within the group? You might also note if highly organized groups with well-defined codes (e.g., the military service, unionized-employee groups, and sports teams) demonstrate fewer examples of discrimination and segregation.

1. Identify the group you are observing (e.g., class, sports team, or AA group).

2. Give examples of cooperation or noncooperation.

3. Give examples of prejudice and/or stereotyping (or nonprejudicial, nonstereotypical) behaviors.

4. If you could make a suggestion to improve the group's functioning relative to prejudice/stereotyping (or simply improve upon what is already "good"), what would you suggest?

SUMMARY OF SECTION IV
Awareness and Knowledge of Sociopolitical Issues

Reflect on the information discovered in Section IV and identify the most critical ideas relevant to:

1. Your self-identity.

2. Your cross-cultural relationships.

3. Expanding your contacts with different others.

4. Suggestions for increasing your multicultural knowledge.

5. List ideas you should be critically cautious about (i.e., identify biases you have discovered).

6. Based on your work in Section IV, what message, idea, perception about multiculturalism would you like to share with yourself or your colleagues at this time?

7. List any newly discovered sources from which you obtained information of a multicultural nature.

SOURCE (book, film, etc.)	NATURE/TYPE OF SOURCE	WHERE TO FIND IT (address, phone, etc.)
1.		
2.		
3.		
4.		
5.		
6.		
7.		
8.		

V

Getting Ahead in the United States

Background Reading: Chapter 6, "Education and Achievement," and Chapter 7, "Work and Career Development," in John A. Axelson, *Counseling and Development in a Multicultural Society* (3rd ed.). Pacific Grove, Calif.: Brooks/Cole, 1999.

FOR YOUR CONSIDERATION

"Achieving the American Dream" is a phrase recognized by most citizens of the United States. It speaks to the notion that all people living here have the right to pursue maximizing their potential and acquiring the rewards of this society. To some degree this notion assumes that hard-working people can overcome most, if not all, obstacles that stand in their way—and we do have many examples that appear to make this point. Nevertheless, do you believe that all U.S. citizens can "achieve the dream" by simply "working hard"? Are there conditions and/or influences that cannot be overcome by simple hard work?

ALSO FOR YOUR CONSIDERATION

Assuming the *quality* and *amount* of one's formal education positively influence one's upward mobility, what conditions or influences in U.S. society impact most negatively on upward mobility (i.e., work to counteract educational achievement)? Are there also internal (as opposed to external) processes and experiences within a cultural group that may impede progress? Can an individual or group be so experientially isolated from participation in upward mobility processes and/or dreams that conceptualizing greater possibilities is nigh impossible? As related to these issues, what is the actual leadership role for those who have "made it" versus those who have not?

A variety of reasons account for the success of individuals, indeed whole cultural groups, throughout the history of the United States. Also, many factors have made upward mobility a difficult task for many citizens. Prejudice—in the form of a variety of "isms," discriminatory practices, and biases—continues to be problematic for many. Nevertheless, the single most important factor in accessing the good life and gaining upward job mobility appears to be directly related to educational achievement. Parents, educational leaders, politicians, and others persistently ask for improvement in the entire enterprise of education. Indeed, economically as well as philosophically, "we cannot afford to waste a single person."

Education has not only been a cornerstone of and vehicle for social and economic advancement, but the school experience has also served as one of the primary socialization processes for participants in this society. The educational enterprise (most likely the single largest production effort in the United States) has been called upon to provide the necessary knowledge and preparation for work and career in a rapidly changing society. It is also increasingly recognized as critical to encouraging the development of the social and psychological characteristics necessary for living in a pluralistic nation. It is rare today for any level of educational system—elementary, secondary, and postsecondary—not to celebrate in some fashion multiculturalism or diversity.

Educational systems, through the totality of their curricula (courses, sports, club activities, events, and human interactions) prepare and educate the next generation for participation in the society at large. In addition to specific academic content, learners develop understandings about achievement, success or failure, possible career roles and directions, societal and cultural expectations, individual and group relationship skills, and social values and beliefs that will affect them and this society for the rest of their lives.

However, we must also recognize that our personal shaping begins prior to entering formal educational systems, prior to entering the workplace. That is, our understandings of others and our ability to relate to others have their beginnings in experiences within our family and cultural group. Within these systems, whether formally or informally, we knowingly or unknowingly learn ways of relating to others, working with others, valuing or not valuing others. Learning concepts of right and wrong, fair treatment, appreciating differences, equality, what we can get away with and not get away with, competition and cooperation are not only presented to us intellectually but are amplified and reinforced in how we are treated and are told or shown how to treat others. We have already been taught (and learned) certain views toward self and others for five or six years prior to starting formal education. However, at such an early age and continuing particularly in our early formal educational experience, we are not always aware of nor in control of what is presented. Given the subtlety (granted it may not be intentionally negative) and the persuasiveness of the presenter/teacher (father, mother, sibling, teacher), we often do not question what is learned except when it is of an extreme and obvious nature; that is, when it is in clear conflict with what we know to be right or correct. Thus, what we know about others, about fairly treating, appreciating, and valuing others, is often based on ideas that have their origins in family- and culture-centered understandings and beliefs.

Such perspectives of self and others are then further reinforced, albeit usually with modification, in school and workplace experiences. The encouragement of "not wasting a single person" in the context of this pluralistic and rapidly changing society suggests a reexamination of what we have learned about self and others in all of these experiences.

FOR YOUR CONSIDERATION

The following chart identifies selected items drawn from the 1992 and 1996 *Statistical Abstract of the United States*. Notice that both the U.S. and world population projections indicate a "doubling" of inhabitants. By the year 2050, some predictions identify that the world population will be close to 25 billion—that is, 5 persons for every 1 that populates the earth today! If not you, many of your children and certainly your grandchildren will be right in the middle of this phenomena. How will the resources be shared, who will do the deciding, what kind of home will your children live in, will your daughter earn as much as your son, what will be the status/nature of social welfare programs including such things as national health care, social security, and so on?

	1990	1991	2000	2010	2025
USA Population	248,700,000	252,700,000	268,266,000	282,575,000	365,000,000
World Population	5,329,407,000	5,422,908,000	6,284,643,000	7,239,935,000	11,500,000,000

Religious Preferences, 18 years and older	Protestant	Catholic	Jewish	Other	None
(1990)	56%	25%	2%	6%	11%
(1994)	60%	24%	2%	6%	8%

Highest Degree Earned, 25 years and older	High School no degree	High School degree	College no degree	College with degree		
				Associate's	Bachelor's	Advanced Degree
(1987)	22.5%	36.6%	17.6%	6.3%	12.2%	5.1%
(1995)	18.3%	33.9%	17.6%	7.1%	15.2%	7.8%

Poverty Thresholds	1 person	2 persons	3 persons	4 persons	5 persons	9+ persons
(1990)	$6,652	$8,509	$10,419	$13,359	$15,792	$26,848
(1994)	$7,547	$9,661	$11,821	$15,141	$17,900	$30,300

Number of families below poverty level: 7.1 million = 10.7% of families in 1990; 8.1 million = 11.6% of families in 1994.

Number of persons below poverty level: 33.6 million = 13.2% of USA in 1990; 38.1 million = 14.5% of USA in 1994.

Income in $	0–9,999	10,000–14,999	15,000–24,999	25,000–34,999	35,000–49,999	50,000–74,999	75,000+
Percent of Families Earning (1990)	9.4	7.5	16.4	16.2	20.1	18.2	12.2
Percent of Families Earning (1993)	9.6	7.2	15.5	14.8	17.9	19.4	15.5
Percent of Individual Males Earning (1990)	25.1	12.8	21.7	29.2		7.3	3.9
Percent of Individual Males Earning (1993)	24.0	12.4	20.8	28.8		8.7	5.2
Percent of Individual Females Earning (1990)	49.7	14.7	19.0	14.3		1.7	0.6
Percent of Individual Females Earning (1993)	46.4	14.4	19.1	16.5		2.6	0.9

1991 and 1995 MEDIAN SALES PRICE of SINGLE FAMILY HOMES

		USA	NORTHEAST	MIDWEST	SOUTH	WEST
New Built	(1991)	$120,000	$155,000	$110,000	$100,000	$142,300
	(1995)	$133,900	$180,000	$134,000	$124,500	$141,400
Existing	(1991)	$100,300	$141,900	$77,000	$88,900	$147,200
	(1995)	$112,900	$136,900	$93,600	$97,700	$147,200
Mobile Homes	(1991)	$27,800	$30,500	$27,600	$24,500	$38,600
	(1995)	$36,300	$37,500	$36,700	$33,900	$46,900

DISABLED POPULATIONS

A large number of figures exist for estimating the total population of disabled persons in the United States. There is an enormous array of faces to the population of disabled persons in the USA. Thus, only an approximate "guesstimate" is made and one must be careful in considering these number (as of 1991).

Permanently Disabled for Physical Reasons	10,000,000–11,000,000
Disabled for Emotional/Psychological Reasons	14,000,000–15,000,000
Disabled for Developmental Reasons	5,000,000–6,000,000
Disabled for Reasons primarily associated with Age	5,000,000–6,000,000
Disabled for other short/long-term Physical/Mental Reasons	9,000,000–10,000,000
TOTAL	43,000,000–48,000,000 persons = 17%–19% of USA

1992 SOCIAL WELFARE SPENDING: $1.3 BILLION, 21% GROSS NATIONAL PRODUCT

	Social Insurance	Public Aid	Health and Medical	Veterans Programs	Education all levels	Housing Programs	Other
State, Local, and Federal Welfare in Millions	617	208	70	35	292	21	22

Average monthly aid to families with dependent children in 1990 was $392 per month, and in 1994 was $378 per month.

ACTIVITY V-1
How Do You Relate to the Educational Experience?

Imagery

Imagery is both the process and the product of imagination. It can be used as a way to better understand the nature of the educational experience, both for yourself and for others. Common daydreaming usually contains visual images of past events, how you would like things to be, or your anticipation of future experiences. Flights of visual fantasy are characteristic of all people and are a primary way to tap the potential within our subconscious. When openly accepted and subjectively used, the impressions can be helpful in problem solving, learning, comprehending, and personal achievement. That part of you that is glimpsed is probably that which is most personally relevant for what you are seeking. The information usually transcends time and space, is nonlinear, and consists of knowledge beyond our normal concept.

To help you get into a visualization, take a few deep breaths and relax as you exhale. Lengthen the inhaling and exhaling a bit more each time, trying to equalize the duration of inhaling and exhaling.

Family and Culture as an Educational System

Visualize yourself in your family of origin; that is, attempt to recall your early family experiences when some family member was trying to teach you something. Also, attempt to recall the times you watched other members learning about or working on some project. Some examples might include baking a cake, decorating the house for a holiday or birthday, a sibling or parent studying, painting a room, paying the bills, or just relaxing after a long, hard day.

1. Have you ever thought of your parents, grandparents, siblings, aunts, uncles, cousins, or significant others who raised you or with whom you related as being your *teachers?* List them by family role (e.g., mother, brother, uncle, and so on) and recall an example of a project where they were your teacher.

FAMILY ROLE	PROJECT

2. What did your family teach you about:

   a. The value of learning (something, anything).

b. The value of working.

c. The ways and means of being successful.

d. The ways and means of cooperating with others.

e. The ways and means of competing with others.

f. Who deserves opportunity.

g. Who doesn't deserve opportunity.

h. What the characteristics of a good worker are.

i. What the characteristics of a bad worker are.

j. How employers should (or do) treat employees.

k. How you should treat employees.

1. The purpose of work.

m. The purpose of life.

n. How to approach learning.

o. How to approach working.

p. How to act toward those who are your supervisors (e.g., father, mother, older siblings, older persons, employers, etc.).

3. Over your early years, say from birth until 18–20 years of age, can you recall:

a. How other persons of your cultural heritage reinforced these family teachings?

b. How other persons of your cultural heritage challenged these family teachings?

4. Can you recall how specific others *not* of your cultural heritage:

   a. Reinforced these family teachings?

   b. Challenged these family teachings?

5. Can you identify how (then or now) the general society at large:

   a. Reinforced these family teachings?

   b. Challenged these family teachings?

6. Can you recall any specific or general family teachings, culture teachings, or society-at-large teachings about how persons *not* of your racial or ethnic background relate to learning or working? Identify these on the chart below.

RACIAL/ETHNIC GROUP	RELATE TO LEARNING	RELATE TO WORKING

ACTIVITY V-2
What Were Your Own Formal Schooling Experiences Like?

Picture yourself in front of the grade school you attended. Look around. You can see the playground and the equipment and the children. You enter the door and go into the hallway. Close your eyes and let your imagination guide you for as long as you desire. . . . (Later, for another visualization, you might want to imagine that you are in high school. What do you see? Or visualize what college was/is like.) Can you see yourself? What are you doing? Take your time.

Thoughts and Questions

Let your imagination flow through you, getting glimpses of your remembered early school life. If you're doing this activity with others, let each person share his or her images. Don't try to interpret. Just tell about your experience and then listen to what others have to express.

You don't have to answer all the following questions, just let them aid your focusing:

1. What images did you see, or do you still see right now?

2. What feelings do you have?

3. Was the experience happy, painful, troublesome, strange, or puzzling?

4. What were you doing?

5. Were other people in your visualization? What were they doing?

6. Did similar events, situations, or people seem to recur?

7. What meaning do you attach to your visualization?

8. What would you like to continue, or finish, if you could do the same visualization over again?

9. If you could change something about your visualization, what would it be?

10. Do any of these recollections/visualizations affirm or disconfirm early family or cultural teachings?

   a. Reinforcing examples:

   b. Challenging examples:

ACTIVITY V-3
Peers and Classmates of Difference

1. Identify peers (classmates, playmates) you recollect or know now who represent a racial/ethnic/cultural group different from your own. Start with your earliest schooling experiences and work your way up to the present. Use the following chart.

	PRESCHOOL	KINDERGARTEN	ELEMENTARY	JUNIOR HIGH	HIGH SCHOOL	COLLEGE
1.						
2.						
3.						
4.						
5.						

2. List on the chart that follows these peers and classmates according to their race/ethnicity and sex and age.

HERITAGE	NAME	MALE/FEMALE	AGE
African			
Asian			
Hispanic			
Native American			
White			

3. The above listings give some indication of your exposure to people of difference who were/are essentially your peers—that is, who shared the status of student/classmate with you.

    a. Are there any patterns that emerge?

    b. What might these patterns of early and/or current exposure to people of difference mean to you today?

ACTIVITY V-4
Teachers, Administrators, and Others of Difference

1. Identify teachers, teacher aides, parent volunteers or tutors, and professors you recollect or know now who represent a racial/ethnic/cultural group different from your own. Start with your earliest schooling experiences. Use the chart below.

	PRESCHOOL	KINDERGARTEN	ELEMENTARY	JUNIOR HIGH	HIGH SCHOOL	COLLEGE
1.						
2.						
3.						
4.						
5.						

2. Identify school social workers, counselors, and psychologists you knew or know who represent a racial/ethnic/cultural group different from your own. Start with your earliest schooling experiences. Use the chart below.

	PRESCHOOL	KINDERGARTEN	ELEMENTARY	JUNIOR HIGH	HIGH SCHOOL	COLLEGE
1.						
2.						
3.						
4.						
5.						

3. Identify principals, assistant principals, deans or other school administrators you knew or know who represent a racial/ethnic/cultural group different from your own. Start with your earliest schooling experiences. Use the chart below.

	PRESCHOOL	KINDERGARTEN	ELEMENTARY	JUNIOR HIGH	HIGH SCHOOL	COLLEGE
1.						
2.						
3.						
4.						
5.						

4. Identify cooks, janitors, school crossing guards or other such personnel you knew or know now who represent a racial/ethnic/cultural group different from your own. Start with your earliest schooling experiences. Use the chart below.

	PRESCHOOL	KINDERGARTEN	ELEMENTARY	JUNIOR HIGH	HIGH SCHOOL	COLLEGE
1.						
2.						
3.						
4.						
5.						

5. Now after reviewing your listings on the charts above, list these people "of difference" by their race/color (in column 1), by their ethnicity/nationality (in column 2), by their sex (in column 3), by their role/position (in column 4), and by other factors of difference (handicap, priest, nun, etc.) (in column 5). Keep persons grouped. For example:

1. Asian, Chinese, male, counselor

2. Asian, Japanese, female, social worker

3. White, Irish, male, teacher, in a wheelchair

4. White, Italian, female, assistant principal, and so on

Add to the chart if necessary.

	RACE	ETHNICITY	SEX	ROLE/POSITION	OTHER FACTORS (identify)
1.					
2.					
3.					
4.					
5.					
6.					
7.					
8.					
9.					
10.					

6. Can you identify any patterns? Consider the questions below and summarize your data according to the categories named.

   a. Imagine yourself to be 5 or 6 years old again. What would your impressions be, given:
   (1) Who the teachers, aides, and professors are?
   (2) Who the counselors, social workers are?
   (3) Who the administrators are?
   (4) Who the service personnel are?

   b. Imagine yourself to be 11 or 12 years old again. What would your impressions be, given:
   (1) Who the teachers, aides, and professors are?
   (2) Who the counselors, social workers are?
   (3) Who the administrators are?
   (4) Who the service personnel are?

   c. Imagine yourself to be 16 or 17 years old again. What would your impressions be, given:
   (1) Who the teachers, aides, and professors are?
   (2) Who the counselors, social workers are?
   (3) Who the administrators are?
   (4) Who the service personnel are?

7. In regard to Activities V-3 and V-4:

   a. Can you recall any particular incidents (experiences or persons involved in your educational history) that taught you anything about cross-cultural relationships? Do you recall any classmates of a different culture being treated differently from you? Did you perhaps feel you were treated differently? Given classmates, teachers, administrators who were/are different from you, did your parents teach you anything about these different people? What did teachers teach you? What did counselors teach you? What did administrators teach you? What did service personnel teach you?

b. Based on these teachings, what did you learn about persons different from yourself? List the different people you have been exposed to in your schooling and summarize what you learned about them as representatives of their culture/heritage. Consider such things as: How did they behave? What did they like? What kinds of personality did they have? What kind of careers did they seek/are suited for? What did you like about them? Dislike about them? What difficulties did you have with them? What positive or negative things happened with them?

    (1) Group: _____ . What I learned: _____

    (2) Group: _____ . What I learned: _____

    (3) Group: _____ . What I learned: _____

    (4) Group: _____ . What I learned: _____

c. Based on your educational experiences, are you aware of any prejudice, discrimination, or bias you or others displayed toward a "different other"
    (1) Because of their race or ethnicity?
    (2) Because of their sex?
    (3) Because of some other characteristic?

d. Given your current age and "looking back" over your educational experiences, what are your impressions? Are you as prepared as you should be for a pluralistic society? What would you do to ensure a better preparation for living and working in this multicultural society? List your ideas of what should be included in *every* student's educational experience.

IN ACADEMIC STUDIES	IN SOCIAL EXPERIENCES

e. Discuss and compare your educational experience with a person of a different race, ethnicity, or cultural grouping. What was similar or dissimilar?

(1) Similar:

(2) Dissimilar:

f. Ask a person of difference to identify what should be included in every student's learning experience (as in d above).

IN ACADEMIC STUDIES	IN SOCIAL EXPERIENCES

g. Compare your responses in d to their responses in f. What have you discovered? If there are differences, what are they and can such different ideas be easily meshed with yours?

ACTIVITY V-5
Working with Others of Difference

Just as we have learned about people of different backgrounds and cultures through our family and educational experiences, the world of work also brings us into contact with many other kinds of people. Identify the first three jobs/positions (including volunteer experiences) you have had and the one you currently have, then list the different kinds of people you have come into contact with in each of them.

JOB/POSITION   COWORKERS OF DIFFERENCE

1st _____   _____

                                                         _____

                                                         _____

                                                         _____

2nd _____   _____

                                                         _____

                                                         _____

                                                         _____

3rd _____   _____

_____

_____

_____

Current _____   _____

_____

_____

_____

1. What did you learn in your work experiences from people who have some aspect of difference from you? Were problems on the job viewed differently from how you viewed them? Were different approaches used in solving problems? Was there a sense of different values or ethics being expressed? What do you recall?

   1st Job:

   2nd Job:

   3rd Job:

   Current Job:

2. Did you learn any particularly useful tactics or strategies of working with different others? Identify the groups represented by your coworkers and the tactic or strategy learned.

   Group: _____ Tactic/strategy: _____

   _____

   Group: _____ Tactic/strategy: _____

   _____

   Group: _____ Tactic/strategy: _____

   _____

   Group: _____ Tactic/strategy: _____

   _____

3. Was it of help or hindrance (given your job and position) to have such diversity in the workforce? Give an example and explain.

4. Can you identify what were, if any, the major differences between you and these different others in getting the job done?

5. Were any of your answers in Questions 1–4 useful in working with other individuals from these other cultural groups? In what ways?

6. Does (did) the nature of the supervisory relationship have anything to do with your views or learnings; that is, were you the supervisor, a supervisee, or in the same position relative to this different other? Does that make a difference in how people relate in a work situation?

ACTIVITY V-6
Types of Work Ethics

One of the most important experiences in the lives of most people is the development of a work ethic. An ethic is a set of values that guide us in dealing with what is good and bad and with duty and obligation. In your work you discover how you want to be treated for how you perform. It's a different experience for everyone. What do you believe at this point in life? Identify your primary views below or assign percentages; for example, 30% of workers are "like this," 40% are "like this," and so on.

_____ 1. Some people don't care how good their work is as long as they are getting paid for the job.

_____ 2. Some people take pride in their work and consider payment a minor or secondary thing.

_____ 3. Still others feel that performance depends on payment. If they are paid well, they will do a good job.

What set of values is associated with/comprises your own work ethic? List three values you believe are most indicative of a good work ethic.

1.

2.

3.

ACTIVITY V-7
What Is Important in Your Work and Career?

Is work an end goal in itself, or is work a means to your well-being? Is career development a process that gets you a series of well-paying, good jobs throughout life? Or is career development the development of an inner you, a self that transcends the jobs you hold and the roles you perform over a lifetime? What conditions are significant to the quality of your life and how do you achieve them? Because our culture is pluralistic, there is no real societal consensus of for a definition of quality of life. The following two exercises are intended to help you examine your own beliefs, feelings, and convictions about what might seem to be important for your own life career and your relations with others.

Self-Assessment of Quality of Life: What You Want to Avoid

It seems easier to measure those things that detract from our welfare than those that add to it. Most people can tell what causes discontent in life and attempt to move away from it. What do you believe or feel is most important for you to avoid in order for you to have a life of quality? Within each column, rank order the following conditions and fears in their order of gravity for you. Your number 1 ranking would be what you would most want to avoid, number 2 would be next most to avoid, and so on.

Have you done anything specific to avoid any of the conditions or fears listed? Identify an example of your response to something you *most* want to avoid.

Example: _____

_____

CONDITIONS TO AVOID

___ poverty

___ hunger

___ sickness

___ illiteracy

___ inadequate housing

___ unemployment

FEARS TO AVOID

___ accidents

___ personal attack

___ war

___ burglary

___ natural disasters

___ toxic and hazardous substances in the environment

Self-Assessment of Quality of Life: What Is Important to You?

It is more difficult to define or measure the ingredients that might constitute quality of life because what is desirable is different for each person and for groups of people. What is it that really makes life pleasant or self-fulfilling at all levels of development?

How can a quality life be developed? When people have freedom from economic cares, they have more choices to make in how to occupy their leisure. What values are important to you? How can you direct your life? Where are you in your own life development?

1. Quickly check (✓) at least five items in *each of* the following two columns that you can relate to and that you believe and feel are most important to you at this time in your life. Then rank the items you checked in order of importance. (1 = most important, 2 = next most important; etc.)

FOR SOCIETY

_____ controlled rates of change in the economy

_____ strong national military defense

_____ public programs

_____ unity of national mission and purpose

_____ humanistic interest, concern, and care for one another

_____ prevention of damage to the environment

_____ quality of life as determined by government action and intervention (government policy)

_____ equal claim by all groups and individuals to some standard requirements for a decent life

_____ collective well-being

_____ compassion, openness, humanness

_____ social well-being through better interpersonal group relations

_____ good jobs for those who strive for them

_____ better housing

FOR YOURSELF

_____ financial wealth

_____ giving up material goods

_____ personal contentment, happiness, and well-being

_____ family life first, work life second

_____ work life first, family life second

_____ knowing yourself

_____ more material goods

_____ individual well-being through better interpersonal relations

_____ access to education at all levels

_____ access to high-paying jobs and opportunities

_____ taking personal risks

_____ increased affluence

_____ higher needs—being, growing, relating

FOR SOCIETY

____ more products at lower prices

FOR YOURSELF

_____ reluctance to join the rat race

_____ quality in living, rather than quantity in living

_____ to live wisely, agreeably, and well

_____ satisfaction of basic needs (food, clothing, shelter)

_____ growth, esteem, freedom, pleasure of meaningful relationships and meaningful work

_____ compassion, openness, and humanness

2. Do you perceive any disrepancies or difficulties between ideas that you believe are important "For Society" versus "For Yourself"? What is the nature of the discrepancy or difficulty if any?

FOR YOUR CONSIDERATION

Finding some higher purpose or meaning in work and in relations with others seems to come to some people only after they have spent years denying or being denied the opportunity to develop compassion, openness, and humanness through their work. Work can be viewed as a means of transforming people, rather than people being transformed by work. For many of us, learning to care *through* our work helps mend the split that has occurred between who we are and what we do on a job. The "workaholic" and "organization person," who compulsively engage in their work, attempt to find meaning by working at a job. A job is not you, nor are you only your specific achievements (an A in a college course or a promotion). Your sense of who you are is carried with you and transcends jobs and the roles you perform. Overemphasis on the need for success will constrict and narrow other possibilities, while perceiving life, work, and career as the same process will give you a sense of wholeness and connectedness with others and life in general.

ACTIVITY V-8
Can You Identify Certain Aspects
of Your Career Development?

Examine each of the following eight statements to see which apply to you. After you read each statement, search for a moment through your educational and vocational experiences and the jobs you have held for examples that might verify the statement. Indicate its applicability to your life with a YES or NO.

1. My life has been, for the most part, an orderly, patterned, and predictable process. Things have happened as I thought they would.

2. My life has been generally unforeseen and unplanned, with a lot of things due to chance and luck.

3. There are things that I could have done, but that it's too late to do anything about now (for instance, learned a specific skill, made a different decision, taken advantage of an experience).

4. I've made some compromises (trade-offs) of things that were important to me in order to get a job or to take advantage of an opportunity.

5. I can see some distinct phases that I have gone through thus far in my career development and tasks that I had to accomplish to get through each phase.

6. I have taken each daily experience for what it might mean, and nothing more. Today is now, and I can't worry about tomorrow or yesterday.

7. I had (have) experiences in which my personal values or interests were (are) not in harmony with others in the culture or work setting.

8. I have a clear picture of my personal, physical, and social needs and desires at this time in my life and of where I am currently in my career development.

Which statements did you relate to most? Which did you relate to least? On the basis of this activity, what do you believe best characterizes your career development pattern thus far in your life?

ACTIVITY V-9
My Current Career Goal

1. Identify your career goal. Describe it as best you can:

   a. The role/position you hope to have or continue in.

   b. The nature of the work, career, and/or occupation.

   c. The type of agency and/or work setting.

2. Do you know any people who are experts in this career (i.e., who already hold such a position as you would like in this occupation)? Identify them by job title and/or position.

3. Comparing yourself to them, what are your

Similarities   Dissimilarities

_____   _____

_____   _____

_____   _____

_____   _____

4. What are the knowledge, attitudes, and skills necessary to being *generally* successful in this position/occupation? Ask your experts to identify these characteristics. That is, what do they have that has made them successful?

	THEY IDENTIFIED	WHAT I HAVE	WHAT I NEED TO DEVELOP
Knowledge			
Attitudes			
Skills			

5. In terms of these characteristics, what have your experts discovered as essential or critical to being successful when working with people who are ethnically/racially different from themselves? List these characteristics below.

    a.

    b.

    c.

6. In terms of "working cross-culturally," what is their major piece of advice?

    a. How well does this advice fit with your own efforts to be successful?

    b. What might you do to develop yourself in regard to this advice?

ACTIVITY V-10
What if You Were the Counselor
in a Culturally Diverse School?

First, take time to do the same deep-breathing exercise that you did in the earlier activities. Relax.

Imagine that you are a counselor and you are walking in the hallway of a school. A group of five students approaches you: one is White, one Black, one Hispanic, one Asian, and one Native American. They are all talking at once, except for the Black student, who is quiet and looks down at the floor. The hall is crowded, so you invite them into your office to discuss what is on their minds. . . . Close your eyes and let the general image take effect for three to four minutes. Open your eyes and quickly jot down on paper what you visualized.

1. What happened in your visualization?

2. What did they say?

3. What did they do?

4. What did you say?

5. What did you do?

6. What were each of the students like?

7. How did you see yourself?

8. How did you feel?

9. Share your impressions with two or three others, preferably from cultural groups different from your own. What are their reactions?

Thoughts and Questions

1. Which one or two impressions stand out most in your mind?

2. What might these impressions personally mean to you?

3. Is there something you really like about what you said or did?

4. Is there something you would like to change in what you said or did?

Perhaps you have to develop a better feeling for a multicultural educational setting. If you think so, visit a school and take in all the impressions you can. Interview students, teachers, administrators, and counselors about the educational experience. Ask some parents what their feelings and thoughts are about school for their children. What is important to them? What changes would they like to see?

More Thoughts and Questions

You might call several businesses, companies, or corporations that employ a diverse workforce. Ask them to identify the issues of a multicultural workforce. What are the positives and negatives they encounter? How do they address these issues? Speak to supervisors, department heads, personnel directors, and regular employees. List issues, ideas, suggestions below.

1.

2.

3.

4.

5.

6.

SUMMARY OF SECTION V
Getting Ahead in the United States

Now reflect on the information you discovered in the foregoing activities. Identify the most critical ideas relevant to:

1. Your self-identity.

2. Your cross-cultural relationships.

3. Expanding your contacts with different others.

4. Suggestions for increasing your multicultural knowledge.

5. List ideas you should be critically cautious about.

6. Based on your work in Section V, what message, idea, perception about multi-culturalism would you like to share with yourself or your colleagues at this time?

7. Now list any newly discovered sources from which you could obtain information of a multicultural nature.

SOURCE (book, film, etc.)	NATURE/TYPE OF SOURCE	WHERE TO FIND IT (address, phone, etc.)
1.		
2.		
3.		
4.		
5.		
6.		
7.		
8.		

VI

Growth and Development

Background Reading: Chapter 8, "Social and Personal Growth," in John A. Axelson, *Counseling and Development in a Multicultural Society* (3rd ed.). Pacific Grove, Calif.: Brooks/Cole, 1999.

FOR YOUR CONSIDERATION

The aspects of the culture and the society we grow up in change over time. For example, our grandparents grew up in a different era and a "different world" than we did. Many formal and informal organizations, as well as movements (such as civil rights), are developed in each era to address the changing world of that generation. Some of these organizations and movements may become a "cultural constant" in the lives of each new generation of a specific cultural group as well as the society as a whole. For example, the church became and served as a resource for immediate help, support, and leadership for African Americans in times of stress. Often such organizations or movements continue addressing human issues and needs in ways that transcend the issues of the earlier time. These organizations often play a powerful role in personal and social development. Was there a societal or culture-specific organization that your grandparents could depend on when they were younger? Does such an organization continue to support you and your generation? How has this resource changed over time and what does it mean to your personal and social development today? What might it mean to the generation that follows yours? In a similar vein, is there a particular movement that has significantly influenced your personal and social development? Might it continue to do so in future generations?

Growth and development in the context of a rapidly changing society require us to learn new skills and acquire new outlooks in order to adjust. We are all familiar with a multitude of stress factors in our society—technological and societal change; family, cultural, and social expectations; changes in health and physical status; aging; changes in the community(ies) we live in, including geographic and climatic conditions; occupational issues of job and career; the nature of the resources we have at our disposal; and even the nature of our own goals in life. The list could easily fill many pages for any individual.

Notwithstanding the fact that conditions in family, culture, and society may produce stress, these social units are also sources of support. Family and culture generally provide security and safety in times of stress and are also primary sources for identity and self-esteem over the life span. While the rules and mores of the society at large are intended to protect each of us, our families and cultures play a primary role in teaching each individual how to adjust—that is, how to cope with and adapt to the immediate pressures of living in the society. Family- and culture-based patterns of adjusting (as taught and/or encouraged) have developed and evolved over many, many generations. Each generation of a family, a culture, a society has developed both specific and generalized views of the world and the nature of humans. Each of these social units has also identified and selected certain coping and role behaviors in accordance with their worldview. And *today's* way of resolving difficulties is based on or is often similar to the ways our forebears addressed similar issues in their time. Indeed, there are certain cognitive and behavioral themes that have been and are transmitted generation to generation that influence our behavior today.

For example—with due cautions against overgeneralization—suppose our concept of family basically includes only three to five generations: ourselves, our children and parents, and our grandchildren and grandparents. How different might our perspectives and behaviors be as compared to a concept of family that embraces hundreds of years and includes all of our family members, living and dead and even not yet born? How might an issue like "family honor or loyalty" be qualified by such a difference in belief? For example, one culture's concept of family may perceive family honor as involving *only* living members (usually three to four generations). Another culture may conceptualize family honor as involving the living *and all* the ancestors (the dead) as well. In other words, that culture believes that the spirits of the ancestors influence the lives of the currently living.

How might such differences in belief affect actions? What behaviors might be engaged in to make atonement to only the living versus to both the living and the dead? Would family goals and expectations of other family members' behavior be different in the two cultures? Would human issues such as divorce, achievement or education, domestic violence, gender roles, and so on be viewed differently by each culture? Would we each learn to conceptualize and address issues of living differently from the "next person in the next culture"?

Across time and in relation to other available resources and influences (such as the environment, biology, education), different cultural groups have developed different techniques and styles along with particular concepts to address the process of life and living. Indeed, there are many different culture-based notions of what "life" and "living" may be. In the process of living, humans have also generally reinforced (and modified) older patterns of behavior and thought. That is, we likely attempt to solve present difficulties by using behaviors and thinking known to be successful in the past. Furthermore, we will make such effort, doubly so, if our behavior and thinking are also approved or encouraged by our current, living family and cultural group. Not surprisingly, our current behavior is often somewhat reflective of the "way it has been done for generations."

As such, while we act as individuals in response to our immediate experience, we are rarely independent of the subtle and not so subtle influences of the generations of family and culture that have preceded us. We may be differentially influenced by those ideas and approved ways of being that have quite a history of development and importance within our culture. Our development, in spite of what we may like to believe, is not the result of behaviors, beliefs, and attitudes that have been created overnight. Our individual growth and development occur in the context of family and cultural history. For example, a particular value may be important to many different peoples; yet the expressing of the value may be quite different from group to group. Most cultures, for instance, value the concept that individuals should exercise some control in their life. However, the concept of individual control and the behavioral expression of "being in control" often vary tremendously from culture to culture. For example, "be quiet, it'll go away" and "shout and scream" may both be behaviors that address a sense of control or being in control. However, few would argue about the difference in these two ways of expressing oneself. Can you think of a culture that might be characterized by one or the other of these behavioral modes of resolving differences? Be careful not to overgeneralize or rigidly stereotype, even though it may appear that cultural groups seem to choose one manner or approach to solving problems. As mentioned before, if a behavior is commonly understood, accepted, and practiced throughout a culture, if you were raised in that culture, it would be somewhat unusual for you to act differently. And, if this is how things are commonly resolved within the culture, a speedy and reasonable resolution is more likely as opposed to using an approach that is unusual or "not the way things are done."

The following exercises ask you to review many of your own specific developmental experiences. You are asked to identify how you might have developed if your experiences had been different. In these explorations we suggest that you try to identify what you learned from those experiences. We also ask you to imagine the knowledge, understandings, attitudes, and behaviors that seem to transcend your own experience. That is, try to identify commonalities that are shared only with other members of your family and those characteristics that are common throughout your cultural heritage group. Then, compare these qualities or aspects of your culture with persons or families of different heritage? One more suggestion we share is that you not attempt to discover or identify all the "exceptions" (i.e., the individual or singular rationale for explaining a behavior or idea in a specific instance). Rather, look for tendencies to understand or behave *most of the time* according to a particular point of view. Try to discover the *patterns* of behavior and environmental conditions that support different behaviors from group to group.

Lastly, given that each culture and nation at this juncture of history seems to be changing rapidly, it may appear to be difficult to isolate certain viewpoints or behaviors as indicative of a particular culture. We are increasingly brought into contact with such a variety of different peoples and ideas that it is not easy to always identify where our understandings have originated. Nevertheless, as multicultural as we seem to be becoming, there are few of us who are not influenced by the uniquenesses of our own particular heritage. That heritage or culture and the ways it has influenced us occurs, on the one hand, in the context of our personal and family development experiences. And, on the other hand, these experiences are further defined by the nature of our interactions with people of different cultural heritage as well as the society at large.

ACTIVITY VI-1
Reconstructing Your Early (and Current) Primary Family Experiences

Think Back to Your Own Family of Origin

1. How many brothers and sisters do you have?

2. Did you relate more to one than to the others? Why?

3. What was your place in the birth order: first, middle, last, only child?

4. Were you adopted?

5. Do (did) you have two parents in your family? a stepparent? half-brothers, half-sisters?

6. Do (did) relatives live with your family?

7. Do (did) your family and relatives visit each other?

8. Do (did) you have family reunions of relatives? How often?

9. What are (were) they like?

10. Do (did) you have a special relative whom you admired (uncle, aunt, grandparent, cousin)?

11. What made the person seem special to you?

12. What do you remember of the stresses and conflicts that your family experienced?

13. What are (were) some pressures on you that you can remember?

14. Did you ever wish that your life would end or want to run away from your family?

15. What were the circumstances that made you feel that way?

16. What pressures do you believe your parents had? your brothers and sisters?

What about the Cultural Environment Where You and Your Family Lived?

If you lived in a number of neighborhoods while growing up, think of those that seem to stand out the most in your mind.

1. Was your neighborhood located in an urban city area, rural area, suburban area, small town, large town?

2. Was it an old, established neighborhood, a new neighborhood, a changing neighborhood?

3. Was it a neighborhood of ethnic families, mixed groups?

4. What were the other families like: different from yours, like yours, kept to themselves, friendly, helpful?

5. What do you believe was the general socioeconomic level of your family and other families in your neighborhood?

6. Were there elderly persons in your neighborhood?

7. What do you remember about them?

8. What spare-time activities did you and the other neighborhood kids engage in?

9. Do you recall "special" adults whom you liked or admired in your neighborhood?

10. What about them did you admire or like?

Where Are You Now?

Now conduct a current exploration of your family-self by restating Questions 1–16 (Family of Origin) to explore either (a) current relationships with members of your family of origin or (b) how your current family living situation may be different from the one you grew up in. Also restate Questions 1–10 (Cultural Environment) to explore what is different in your current environment as compared to the one you grew up in. For example, Question 2 (Family of Origin) could be restated: "Do you currently relate more to one than to the others?" This question could be followed by further questions such as "Has there been a change over the years *and* what is the nature of that change?"

1. Briefly describe your present family situation. Is there a significant difference compared to your childhood? In what ways?

2. Briefly describe your present neighborhood. Is there a significant difference compared to your childhood? In what ways?

3. Identify one significant milestone at each age category of your life that led to your developing (taught you) a particular understanding of life and your relationship to others. Identify what you learned or what was taught to you regarding this experience according to: the event itself, your family, your culture, the society at large.

AT AGE	EVENT	LEARNED FROM EVENT	LEARNED FROM FAMILY	LEARNED FROM CULTURE	LEARNED FROM SOCIETY
0–6					
7–12					
13–20					
21–36					
37–49					
50–62					
63–75					
76+					

4. Examine, compare, and summarize what you learned from each particular milestone; that is, blend the four perspectives together so that you end up with one central theme or understanding learned from each experience that guides your behavior today. List them below.

0–6   a. _____

7–12   b. _____

13–20   c. _____

21–36   d. _____

37–49   e. _____

50–62   f. _____

63–75   g. _____

76+   h. _____

5. Now, if you can, rank them (1 = most important, 2 = next, and so on) according to their importance to you.

6. And now, according to how you *now actually* live your life, rerank these understandings. You might ask yourself, "When it comes right down to it, do I usually act according to *this* understanding?"

7. Does any learning predominate in your practice of living, yet appear to be at odds with the others listed? How do you account for this condition?

8. Is it seemingly impossible to separate one understanding from one or more of the other understandings? What does this suggest?

9. Looking back over your life span, does it seem that you are living in (i.e., influenced by) the past, present, and future simultaneously? Explain.

ACTIVITY VI-2
A Worldview

1. Based on our developmental experiences and what we have learned about ourself as well as others, we often construct a personal perception of what life and living is all about. This may be referred to as our own "worldview." A worldview of self in human relationships could include such qualities as loyal, wonderful, careful, cautious. A worldview of family might include qualities such as close knit, supportive, somewhat distant emotionally. A culture could be viewed as outgoing, reserved, restrictive, flamboyant; and others might be viewed as persons to be trusted, persons to be careful of, and so forth.

   These different views of self, family, culture, and others denote to some degree how we view and approach human relationships. By identifying such perceptions we can become more cognizant of ideas that influence how we behave in relationship to others; that is, with the world at large. As life is a series of *events-in-living,* our worldviews do undergo change. Yet early experiences and what we learned from them often have a pervasive influence over the entire life span.

   It is not uncommon that individuals and/or groups that experience commonalities of developmental experiences also develop a commonality in their "worldviews." Complete the phrases that follow. Record the first thoughts that come to mind— there are no "correct" answers.

   a. I am

   b. My family is

   c. My culture is

   d. Others are

   e. Therefore, the world is

2. Ask three family members to complete the phrases above. What can you make of their answers? Are there commonalities? differences?

3. Ask three other persons of your culture to complete the phrases. What can you make of their answers? Are there commonalities? differences?

4. Ask three persons from each of three different cultures to complete the phrases. What can you make of their answers? Are there commonalities? differences?

5. What might account for the commonalities as well as the differences you have discovered?

6. How can these understandings be useful to you in improving your relationships within your own family or cultural group as well as with other cultural groups?

ACTIVITY VI-3
Multicultural Flexibility

In his *Psychotherapy and Counseling with Minorities* (New York: Pergamon Press, 1991), Manuel Ramirez's approach to multicultural counseling suggests that human diversity and human differentness can be understood from cultural and cognitive perspectives. The healthiest interactions between persons of different heritage seem to occur when there is a shared understanding of the historical and current events that influence the behavior of each person today.

Multicultural Analysis

Complete a brief self-analysis of your personality orientation as based on cultural and cognitive behavior styles. Check the statements that most apply to you (i.e., your tendency to act "like this" rather than "like that" most of the time).

CULTURAL ORIENTATION

Traditional Style

_____ prefer that others take the initiative

_____ expect that people of position should do most of the talking

_____ prefer to be quiet

_____ observant of social environments

_____ focus on others

Modern Style

_____ prefer equal status with others

_____ expect to do as much talking as anyone else

_____ assertive and self-confident

_____ ignore social environment

_____ focus on myself

COGNITIVE ORIENTATION

Field Sensitive Style

_____ self-disclosing

_____ interested in personal relationships

_____ help from others is important

_____ global focus (deductive)

Field Independent Style

_____ depersonalize problems

_____ interested in solving problems

_____ making personal progress is important

_____ detail focus (inductive)

Exploration of Your Self-Analysis

1. What is the general orientation of your personality styles? Do you have more of a *traditional* or more of a *modern* style? More of a *field sensitive* or more of a *field independent* style?

2. Can you think of life examples that demonstrate your orientation?

3. What do you see as your major mode of being (cultural) and of perceiving (cognitive)?

4. Imagine a situation where you need to relate to a person whose orientation is different from yours. What might you expect?

5. Could you be flexible in this situation? What might such flexibility involve?

6. How could you improve your cultural and cognitive flexibility in general?

ACTIVITY VI-4
Assessment of Human Attributes

In all the foregoing exercises thus far in this manual, you have reviewed a wide array of information about yourself, your family, your cultural environment, and the cultural environments of others. You have been developing your understanding of yourself and the world in the context of your experiences. In the chart that follows, you are asked to briefly describe each of the listed attributes for (A) yourself, (B) your family of origin, (C) the generalized others within the same ethnic/socioeconomic cultural group with which you identify, and (D) selected others whose cultural background or experiences are different from yours. Complete columns A, B, and C first.

Then, in column D, ask one to three persons of a different cultural background to share their perception of the personality of your culture, the nature of social relationships within your culture, the achievement orientation of your culture, and so on. If you like, you might also ask three persons of your own cultural background to share their perceptions.

Do not share your own answers prior to others assessing the attributes. Do not expect that they will respond to all the items. Do not expect consistency with your responses because the perception by others is not based on the same specific knowledge you have about such attributes.

ITEM	A MY OWN	B MY FAMILY'S	C MY CULTURE'S	D OTHERS' DESCRIPTION (in reference to your culture)
Personality				
Nature of Social Relationships				
Achievement Orientation				
Control Orientation				
Most Important Value				
General Style of Problem Resolution				
Greatest Strength				
Greatest Weakness				

1. Have you discovered any commonalities; that is, answers that tend to reaffirm your own answers?

2. With whom is there consistency?

3. Are there major differences of perception? With whom?

4. What might account for such differences?

5. Would (do) such differences create problems for you in relating to family members, your culture, society?

6. What could you do about these problems?

ACTIVITY VI-5
Accessing Awarenesses from Life and Living

Each human life is lived in the context of a wide variety of learning experiences. We draw information and understandings about self and others from the nature of these experiences. What we learn is further influenced by how significant others (family, friends, teachers, etc.) react to the experience and/or the persons involved. Sometimes we receive messages that are purposefully and obviously intended for us, but some messages are not obvious—they may even be hidden or unintentional. Often we have an awareness of the information we bring to a situation, but sometimes we do not. Most people agree that what we are *not* aware of is often just as important as what we *are* aware of.

The following "awareness games" may at times vex you, but please bear with us. You may experience reactions that are inconsistent with, even opposite to, how you interrelate with others. Nevertheless, we believe the activities will raise questions that are quite important for your consideration. Awareness, with the questions it raises, is the first step in assessing your attitudes and beliefs, in identifying historical and current information that influence your behavior, and in determining what you might do to improve your relationships.

Games Teach Us about Self and Others

Games, including sports, often have cultural overtones. They have been developed as ways of learning about life as well as for enjoyment. Games like Monopoly, Dungeons and Dragons, cowboys and Indians, playing house, Chinese checkers, football, stickball, soccer, basketball, baseball, or games played with jacks or toy soldiers introduce us to strategies for living as well as suggest what and how we are to think of and relate to others.

1. List the games you have played or still do play. Name or describe the game, any culture(s) it may relate to, the idea of the game, and describe the nature of a good and bad guy and player in the game.

GAME/DESCRIPTION	CULTURE	IDEA OF GAME	"GOOD" GUY/PLAYER	"BAD" GUY/PLAYER
1.				
2.				
3.				
4.				
5.				

2. Who did you want to be when you played the game? Or was there a certain way to play the game if you were to win? Describe this character and/or the "winner's" approach.

3. Were there certain kinds of understandings you developed about life or culture—yours or others'—from these games?

   a. From the game itself?

   b. From the people who played the game with you?

   c. From others (parents, older siblings, teachers, etc.)?

4. Ask some friends of different cultural backgrounds about the games they played (or do play) and what the game rules and character roles suggest. Do you find similarities? If so, what are they?

What's Involved in Name-Calling?

As children we all probably have called other children any number of names and had the "favor" returned. Children generally seem to use terms such as those in the list below to hurt others or defend themselves. Children may know, but often do not know, the derogation of these terms; that is, they use them usually out of anger or ignorance and not out of prejudice or bias. While adults may also speak from ignorance, they usually are expressing not only immediate, personal anger but are also speaking from a context of values and beliefs about other people—that is, from a viewpoint of learned prejudice and/or dislike or even unreasoned fear of certain other kinds of people.

Different kinds of people or characteristics of people come to mind when we hear such names. Over the years we learn, willing or not, words and/or ideas associated with certain terms. While we may intellectually, cognitively know the "rightness" or "wrongness" of such terms and never use them openly, still they are often elements of our internal dialogue. Such hidden uses may address how we view others and even suggest the way we think things should be.

1. What immediately comes to mind when you hear the following terms. That is, what "picture forms in your mind"? Use a few key words to describe the picture.

2. What feelings do you immediately experience (confusion, "yuk," disgust, anger, "right on," "so what," positive, negative, sadness, nothing, etc.)?

TERM	PICTURE	FEELING
White devil		
Oreo		
Slope		
Coon		

TERM	PICTURE	FEELING
Bozo		
Cripple		
Wop		
Bombshell		
Kraut		
Polack		
Savage		
White trash		
Mau Mau		
Banana		
Plastic people		
Preppy		
Shyster		
Hillbilly		
AAAA-rab (Arab)		
Pimp		
Opportunist		
Junkie		
Farmboy		
Racist		
Banker		
Gay		
White bitch		
Stud		
Faggot		
Barbarian		
Gimp		

TERM	PICTURE	FEELING
Greaser		
Lemon		
Spic		
"The Man"		
Sheeny		
Honky		
"Spaszz"		
Homo		
Bohunk		
Kike		
Whitey		
Wetback		
Rag-head		
Mick		
Ghost		
Nigger		
Scammer		
Hun		
Darkie		
Okie		
Dago		
Yuppie		
City slicker		
Old fart		
Bean		
Chink		
Jack pine savage		

TERM	PICTURE	FEELING
Dingo		
Bigot		
Golden boy		
Bimbo		
Tamale		
Wasp		
Uncle Tom		
Can you list other terms?		

3. Have you ever called (or thought of) someone by any of these terms? What were the circumstances?

4. Have you ever been called one of these terms? What were the circumstances?

5. Have you ever heard someone called any of these terms? What were the circumstances?

6. How did you "defend" yourself, or others? What was the end result? How anxious are you to do this again?

7. From whom/where did you learn any of these term? How frequently have you heard, said, or thought any of these terms?

8. How do you feel about seeing and reading these terms?

9. Group the terms as they are stereotyped in your mind with the different groups below.

	EUROPEAN AMERICAN	AFRICAN AMERICAN	ASIAN AMERICAN	HISPANIC AMERICAN	NATIVE AMERICAN	MIDDLE EASTERN AMERICAN	DISABLED AMERICAN
1.							
2.							
3.							
4.							
5.							
6.							
7.							
8.							
9.							
10.							

10. What does the distribution suggest to you about our society? About relations between people of different races or ethnicity or condition or preference status?

11. Circle the terms your family or friends have used when referring to other people. How many years have you heard these words (including their implications) used?

12. Of the groups above, which ones have you had the most difficulty understanding or relating to (or you realize are not very often present among the groups with whom you associate)?

The Other Communities in Town

Almost every city or town has a smaller section that is perceived as either an extremely desirable or undesirable place to live. These sections of town may be perceived as "the wrong (or right side) of the tracks," "the neighborhood we hope to live in someday," or simply a neighborhood where people live who are judged to be different from us or others.

1. Did or does your town have one or more of these neighborhoods? What are they called?

2. The last time you talked about these sections of town, what did you call them? Why?

3. Did (or do) you have a friend who lived or lives on the "wrong" or "right" side of the tracks?

a. What was (is) this relationship like?

b. How important was (is) this relationship to you?

c. What is the most important learning for you from this relationship?

4. What did (or do) others say about this friendship?

a. Family said (says):

b. Friends said (say):

c. Culture says:

d. Society says:

5. What were (are) the characteristics of the people who lived (live) in this part of your town?

6. What do you think living in this part of town "does" to one's:

a. Identity?

b. Treatment by others?

c. Expectations of others?

7. How did (do) you think people who lived in this part of town viewed you? Fairly? unfairly?

8. For what reasons do people end up living on the "other side of the tracks"?

a. What does someone have to do in order to get to that side?

b. What must someone do to be sure he or she doesn't wind up on that side?

9. What stereotypes are associated with people from the wrong side of the tracks? Might they be influencing you today?

10. Talk to one or two people of a different culture about this. What commonalities or differences can you discover?

Fears

Especially when we are children, but also throughout our lives, people often try to frighten us about different things. Sometimes it is about other kinds of people or about certain kinds of situations. Sometimes it may be done "for the good of the child," and sometimes there may be other reasons why people try to scare children or other adults. Explanations may be to maintain the status quo or to protect from perceived or imaginary harm.

1. Has anyone ever tried to frighten you? How did that person do this? Record what was said to you.

2. Have you ever scared a young child?

   a. What was the purpose?

   b. How did you do so?

   c. What kind of information did you use?

3. Were certain kinds of people described to you as people to fear or avoid? How were they described (or who were they)?

4. What kinds of disasters were you warned might befall you if you weren't careful around these people?

5. How was it suggested that you could protect yourself from such people? What were you to do to be safe?

6. You're an adult now, but, nevertheless, what kinds of situations or people are you *now not* comfortable with? Is there any relationship between these situations and how adults scared you?

7. Talk to one or two people of a different culture about this. What commonalities or differences can you discover?

The Good and the Bad and What I Wish I Had

There are many groups of people in the world. All groups of people have unique characteristics or abilities that are easy to envy. Many also may have certain attitudes, beliefs, and/or behaviors or live in situations that may not seem desirable. Often what we like or don't like about others is based on stereotypical material.

Identify what you think is generally desirable and what is not desirable about persons from the following heritages. Note that we are talking "in general"; that is, persons identified as Japanese are being viewed by you as representing general Japanese cultural characteristics. Identify a cultural characteristic they possess that you wish you had or could possess. Indicate whether you are talking about a man or a woman of this group. What you perceive as desirable/not desirable should be focused on as a *cultural characteristic of most people belonging to the identified group* as you know of them.

PERSON'S HERITAGE (MAN/WOMAN)	DESIRABLE CHARACTERISTIC	UNDESIRABLE CHARACTERISTIC	GROUP'S CULTURAL CHARACTERISTIC I WISH I HAD
African or Black			
Arab			
Chinese			
Cuban			

PERSON'S HERITAGE (MAN/WOMAN)	DESIRABLE CHARACTERISTIC	UNDESIRABLE CHARACTERISTIC	GROUP'S CULTURAL CHARACTERISTIC I WISH I HAD
English			
Eskimo			
Greek			
Irish			
Israeli			
Italian			
Indian (Asia)			
Japanese			
Mexican			
Native American			
Puerto Rican			
Russian			

1. Circle your top choice of desirable characteristics; that is, circle what you consider the most desirable characteristic.

2. Circle the worst characteristic; that is, circle what you consider the most undesirable characteristic.

3. Circle your top choice of the "wish I hads."

4. How culturally similar to you is the group associated with your top choice of most desirable characteristic.

5. How culturally similar to you is the group associated with the most undesirable characteristic?

6. How culturally similar to you is the group associated with the best "wish I had"?

7. Now, if you *had to be reborn into* one of the groups *but* had your choice of which group you would be born into, which group would be your first choice? your second choice? your third choice? your fourth choice, and so on? Be sure to indicate whether you would choose to be reborn as a man or a woman. There are 15 groups to rank 1st to 15th.

Identify and explain your choices below.

	EXPLANATION OF CHOICE RANKING
Top Five	
1.	
2.	
3.	
4.	
5.	
Middle Five	
6.	
7.	
8.	
9.	
10.	
Bottom Five	
11.	
12.	
13.	
14.	
15.	

8. What do you notice about your choices, your groupings of choices, or your explanations for the rank order you assigned?

9. Ask a family member/person of your culture to also do a 1 through 15 ranking.

10. Ask one or two persons of different ethnic/racial background from you to do a 1 through 15 ranking.

11. Now assume that there are 15 persons (one from each group) with whom you have "fallen in love" and that you would gladly marry any one of them. Given that you are going to live in the United States and that each person meets all of your personal criteria, which person from which group would you choose first, second, and so on? Use a different color pen or pencil from your first ranking.

Rank 1st through 15th and jot down your basic reason regarding each choice. Base your choice of marital partner on the idea of *which marriage would most likely have the least problems* in regard to your family, your culture, and/or society at large.

12. What did you discover?

   a. Which "mixed" marriage do you think would have the most difficulties in this society?

   b. What is the nature of your choices?

   c. Are your choices related to your perception of physical characteristics, group beliefs, values, behaviors, or cultural practices; a group's social or economic status?

   d. Do any patterns to your explanations or reasons emerge?

You're Only as Old as You Feel?

Chronological aging is both physical and psychological. Physical changes do occur, and psychological perceptions of aging may take on different meanings for different people. "Oldness" may even be perceived differently at different age points in our own lives.

1. At what age will/did you see yourself as "old"?

   ____ 25   ____ 45   ____ 65

   ____ 30   ____ 50   ____ 70

   ____ 35   ____ 55   ____ 75

   ____ 40   ____ 60   ____ 80+

   To what age do you expect to live?

   ____ 25   ____ 45   ____ 65

   ____ 30   ____ 50   ____ 70

   ____ 35   ____ 55   ____ 75

   ____ 40   ____ 60   ____ 80+

3. At what chronological age do you believe various populations of people might think a person is "old"? Make your own estimate of what you think they would say; then ask one to three persons from each of the other groups identified on the chart below.

	SOCIETY AT LARGE	AFRICAN AMERICAN	ASIAN AMERICAN	EUROPEAN AMERICAN	HISPANIC AMERICAN	NATIVE AMERICAN	MIDDLE EASTERN AMERICAN
My estimate							
Theirs							

4. What do you see as positive and negative aspects of being old in the United States? How might other groups see the positive and negative aspects of being old? Identify below.

	MY VIEW	AFRICAN AMERICAN	ASIAN AMERICAN	EUROPEAN AMERICAN	HISPANIC AMERICAN	NATIVE AMERICAN	MIDDLE EASTERN AMERICAN
Positive 1.							
2.							
Negative 3.							
4.							

5. If you had only five more years to live, what would you most want to do or accomplish during those five years?

6. What answers to the question "If you had only five more years to live" might persons of the following groups give?

   a. African American:

   b. Asian American:

   c. European American:

   d. Hispanic American:

   e. Middle Eastern American:

   f. Native American:

7. If you find any difference among the groups, how might they be explained?

Rituals for Passages through Life

Rituals play important roles in our lives. Most cultures have several rituals or practices that emphasize the life changes that we all undergo. Births, marriages, and deaths are just some of the events that cultures make note of. Through celebrations of such milestones of living, people transmit a variety of understandings about their heritage. Those outside of any particular culture may also develop perceptions and understandings based only on what they may see or think these celebrations are all about. Since such rituals are usually practiced privately (i.e., they are not performed for the public and usually are within the context of a family gathering), misunderstandings can develop about what the event means as well as about the people celebrating such events.

Rituals are usually performed according to the accumulated experiences, values, and behaviors of a specific culture. Special celebrations can often provide us with deep insights into group culture; that is, what is important to the group and what kinds of behaviors are expected of persons within the culture. While most cultures celebrate many of the same life events—for example, a birth—they have many different ways of expressing its importance. Indeed, there may be several levels of importance attached to births, such as first born versus last born, a boy versus a girl. Groups may also recognize different kinds of events that other groups may not consider important or may view as an odd thing to celebrate.

1. Identify two or three persons of cultural groups different from your own and ask them to help you fill in the chart below. Be prepared to discuss with them the various information they share.

    a. First, in columns A and B, list several events/rituals that are observed within your *own* cultural group and then identify what is significant about these events.

    b. Now ask the persons of each different cultural group to identify if *your* event 1 is also significant within *their* culture and how so. Follow the same procedure for each other event. Record their answers in columns C, D, and E, respectively.

    c. Identify in each event if there is general agreement as to the event's significance, but also identify if there is any difference in the reasons for its significance.

    d. Are there any unique messages given about life and living during these events and their rituals that are different from cultural group to group?

    e. Also, ask these others to identify other events (6–8) that are of particular and unique importance to their cultures and why they are. Do you have any reactions relative to these other events that you would share with your colleagues?

A EVENT/RITUAL IN MY CULTURE	B SIGNIFICANCE OF EVENT/RITUAL	C CULTURE #1 SIGNIFICANCE	D CULTURE #2 SIGNIFICANCE	E CULTURE #3 SIGNIFICANCE
1.				
2.				
3.				
4.				
5.				

A EVENT/RITUAL IN MY CULTURE	B SIGNIFICANCE OF EVENT/RITUAL	C CULTURE #1 SIGNIFICANCE	D CULTURE #2 SIGNIFICANCE	E CULTURE #3 SIGNIFICANCE
6.				
7.				
8.				

2. What kind of similarities/dissimilarities did you discover:

   a. In the description of the event?

   b. In the message for "life and living"?

3. Did you discover any celebrations that seem unusual to you? Was the ritual or the message unusual? In what ways?

4. Did any of the persons you interviewed feel that your own celebrations were unusual? Did they think the rituals or the messages about life were strange or unusual? In what ways?

ACTIVITY VI-6
Identifying Resources and Environments of Personal and Social Development

A variety of resources and environments influence the nature of developmental experiences. The availability of and accessibility to resources and to nourishing environments determine the manner and possibility of finding appropriate solutions to life's concerns as well as affording opportunities for the achievement of maximum potential development. Easily identifiable resources include economic status; cognitive, intellectual, and physical characteristics and abilities; adequate food; housing/

shelter; adequate educational facilities; playgrounds, parks, community centers; health care facilities; places of worship; and, of course, personal health.

Resources may also include intangibles such as values, beliefs, and the nature of the community one resides in (both psychological and structural) and whether it has recreational opportunities, a transportation system, a feeling of community and whether it is a "tolerant or intolerant" community, the crime rate, the rates of employment/unemployment. All these and other resources and environmental conditions affect the quality of life.

The following questions ask you to think about the resources available to you during past and current development stages. Also reflect on the need for any and/or all of such resources and environments being important in the pluralistic and complex society of the United States. In general, most of these resources are available to any person or group in the United States. However, *availability*—the existence of a resource—does not always mean the resource is *accessible to* everyone. Consider this notion of accessibility. Do all persons and groups have reasonable access to what is available? It is helpful to do this exercise with a group of culturally diverse persons.

1. What values or beliefs guide your behavior?

   a. Spiritual beliefs (God, religion) or philosophy of life:

   b. Beliefs about human nature:

   c. Personal values that guide you in everyday life:

2. Are there individuals or groups of people who reinforce/support your beliefs/values and who are readily available to you in times of stress?

   a. Who are they? Relatives? neighbors? coworkers?

   b. Do you have any formalized programs of support (churches, temples)? What are they? How do they provide support?

Another source of support is found in the exemplary behavior of our heroes and heroines. Their actions, writings, and speeches may inspire us in times of stress. Likewise, awards, honors, and recognitions we have received also address (support) our belief in ourself and are often a source of emotional and cognitive support when we need that "extra reminder."

3. Do you have heroes and heroines, real or imagined? Identify them and what they stand for in your mind.

   IDENTITY OF
   HERO/HEROINE   WHAT THEY STAND FOR OR WHAT THEY MEAN TO ME

   a. _____   _____

   b. _____   _____

   c. _____   _____

IDENTITY OF HERO/HEROINE	WHAT THEY STAND FOR OR WHAT THEY MEAN TO ME
d. _____	_____
e. _____	_____
f. _____	_____

4. List awards, recognitions, honors you have received. What do (did) they mean to you? Do (did) they identify the kind of person you are?

AWARDS/HONORS RECEIVED	WHAT THE AWARD MEANS (MEANT) TO ME
a. _____	_____
b. _____	_____
c. _____	_____
d. _____	_____
e. _____	_____
f. _____	_____

5. Are there special documents, sayings, speeches, writings (books, poetry), or experiences that have been especially meaningful and/or serve as a resource/guide in your processes of living?

ITEM/EXPERIENCE	MESSAGE/MEANING
a. _____	_____
b. _____	_____
c. _____	_____
d. _____	_____
e. _____	_____

6. Who are the persons (lay or professional) you have utilized or would utilize to help you if you had a problem?

FAMILY MEMBERS OR RELATIVES	PROFESSIONAL PEOPLE	CLERGY	OTHERS
a. _____	_____	_____	_____
b. _____	_____	_____	_____
c. _____	_____	_____	_____
d. _____	_____	_____	_____

7. What kinds of community agencies/organizations are you aware of and might use if you had a need? For example, what is available to you and to others such as single mothers, the chronically mentally ill, the developmentally disabled, the homeless? Don't forget service organizations like the Lions Club, the Jaycees, the NAACP, and such. The following chart should help you in listing such resources. Comparing your list with another's may make you aware of other resources to address human needs.

HEALTH CARE	PSYCHOSOCIAL	RECREATIONAL	CIVIC	CAREER	EDUCATIONAL

8. What is the nature of your community?

    a. Is it an easy place to live in?

    b. What is most difficult about it?

    c. How does it positively/negatively influence the quality of life?

    d. How might it be a difficult place to live in for youth, elderly, for disabled persons, others?

9. What other resources or environments can you name that you think influence or are critical to people's personal and social development?

10. Now it might be interesting to see what others identify in Questions 1 through 8, especially if you have been working in a group with members of a variety of cultures. What did you discover by comparing your answers with theirs?

ACTIVITY VI-7
Assessing Quality in Human Support Systems

Every human individual and human group usually has a variety of tradition-directed support systems that are dictated by rules, rituals, and relationships derived from past generations and modified only slightly by later generations. These natural support systems contain principles and rules believed to be ideal standards or guides for communities of rational beings.

A family, a culture, a subculture, a community, and a society all generally function as natural support systems. At the very least, natural support systems perform the functions listed in the following chart. Do your support systems perform the functions for you? At what level of quality (+'s = tends to do well, –'s = tends to do not so well; for example, + + + = very well)?

FUNCTIONS	SUPPORT SYSTEMS				
	Family	Culture	Subculture	Community	Society at Large
Collects/disseminates information					
Gives feedback and guidance					
Acts as a source of ideology/beliefs					
Mediates in problem solving					
Recognizes my needs					
Provides concrete and practical aid					
Provides an opportunity for rest and recuperation					
Acts as a reference and control group					
Validates identity					

1. What would be an example of each social unit performing each of the functions (e.g., the family might hold family meetings, provide shelter, and so on)?

2. How does the social unit usually perform its functions?

   a. How and when are decisions made?

   b. How are people notified about pending meetings and decisions?

3. Are there individuals, groups, or cultures within society that you perceive as not having the same quality and/or quantity of natural support systems as other groups? Who are they and what are the implications of this difference?

4. How many other kinds of natural support systems can you think of—in your life or in other lives? How important are they to your life or to other lives?

ACTIVITY VI-8
Thinking about Others' Lives and How They Are Lived: Transcultural Experiential/Simulation Exercises

The nature of resources (intellectual, physical, monetary, social, societal) available *and* accessible to you greatly influences your opportunities to grow and develop. They can and do determine the quality of how we experience life. What we have (or do not have) also influences how others respond to us. Yet we often take our resources for granted and do not readily grasp the depth of their meaning and importance in our lives. It is not unusual to find it difficult to understand others if we have not had similar experiences. How might your life experience—your growth and development—be different if you did not have the resources you do have?

The activities that follow introduce you to life experiences that many Americans have every day of their lives. For many of us, once the activity is over we can retreat to our everyday kind of living. Imagine if you couldn't go back! How would your life be different? What would be the nature of your difficulties? How might your way of thinking of the world and others be different? Would you come to think of yourself differently than you do now? Might you be better prepared to understand and to counsel others by these experiences?

We should also recognize that many of the following issues intersect in our lives; that is, we often experience such problems and/or concerns in multiples and simultaneously. Rarely do we have only one problem, and rarely is a singular problem independent of all the other issues ongoing in our lives. Also, rarely does an answer to any particular problem not have some significant impact on the other elements of our lives. Some of the following life issues may seem to be singularly unique to the individual, but all also have components or aspects that relate to family, culture, subcultural grouping, and the society at large. To wit, we exist within a set of systemically interrelated issues, concerns, and relationships—like the system that is our wristwatch or automobile engine. If one part of that system malfunctions (or even is corrected), the impact is felt throughout the entire system.

In effect, no part is independent of the whole, and the whole is certainly more than just the sum of its parts. For example, a religious belief is more than just our relationship to a deity(ies). In short, our beliefs also "speak to" the ways we perceive and are perceived; they suggest certain ways of relating to others. And, furthermore, such beliefs are usually in some relationship with others' norms or understandings within one's culture and the general society. It would be convenient if we could clearly separate any particular issue in our lives and simply find an answer to it, but that does not seem to be the human experience except in rare instances.

In all of the following activities, keep a journal of the reactions of others. Notice if certain kinds of people seem to relate better than usual to you. Do you relate better than usual to others? Do some persons relate to you less than usual? Are there differences because of race, ethnicity, socioeconomic status/condition? Can you discover any patterns or peculiarities? Do you notice anything that you had not been aware of previously?

The point of the exercise is to become aware of how differences in human characteristics or conditions affect us. These experiences will personally introduce you to ideas, information, and experiences that may be quite different from your own. Some activities may not be reasonably possible for you. When such is the case, try to talk with some people who directly confront this issue daily or with those who work with people who do have to confront the issues related to your exercises.

Many communication theorists believe that the nature, as well as the amount, of the information we receive from others (the environment) is of utmost importance to the choices we make. Thus, attitudes and understandings as well as behaviors are chosen in the context of scanning and assessing the environmental input we receive. We all can recall a time when our behaviors, including attitudes toward others, changed dramatically when (or as) the environment changed. Surely you noticed how others changed toward you at these times in your life.

Journaling Suggestion: We sometimes experience *culture shock* when going out of our own cultural environment or beyond our cultural experiences. Feelings of fear, confusion, discomfort, aloneness, as well as impressions of alienation often accompany such new experiences. We strongly encourage you to keep a journal of your experience to help you identify and address these feelings and thoughts. It should be of further help in deepening your understandings of others' lives to compare your discoveries and reactions with others who also complete the following exercises. A list of questions you might address in a journal are provided below.

Possible Journal Reaction Questions

1. Describe the type of activity. How did you prepare yourself?

2. When and where did you start? At home, on the street, in a neighborhood, at a club, at work?

3. What did you notice about yourself as you did the exercise?

4. What did you notice about others as you did the exercise?

5. What was the most difficult aspect of the exercise for you?

6. Was it easy to ask for help as it was needed? How did that feel?

7. Were others comfortable in giving help? Did they seem to avoid you?

8. What were the nicest things done for/to you? Describe your feelings.

9. What reactions of yourself or others most upset you?

10. Did any reactions seem related to your race, ethnicity, or culture? Related to another's heritage?

11. Summarize what you learned from and about the experience, about others, about yourself.

Cautionary note: Some of the exercises may require the assistance of friends. You might also want to talk to others before trying some of these. We will give you some hints along the way. Whatever you attempt, do not place yourself or others in "harm's way." Do not break the law, and do not violate another's work/life schedule. Given a little information, many people will help you learn what can be learned of a situation. Sometimes you will want to talk it over rather than "do it." Use discretion with your fellow humans; their time is important also. Modify the activity if you must. Journaling your experience and comparing it to another's experiences, as suggested above, may be helpful in sorting out the feelings, impressions, and thoughts you have during the following activities.

EXPERIENTIAL/SIMULATION EXERCISES

(Remember, journaling your experiences may be quite helpful to further your understanding.)

A. It's Only a "Little" More Difficult

You have a handicap: *Try to navigate your daily schedule after you:*

1. Borrow or rent a wheelchair for the day.

2. Borrow or make a white cane for the blind.

3. Hide your writing hand and arm under your coat. Then *do not use it.* Try to dress yourself without using that arm.

Hints: Use public transportation. Try to get a friend to take you everywhere. Go to a restaurant. Do not break the law or jeopardize your own safety. Stay within your neighborhood if you have to.

B. You Can't Read

1. Visit a grocery store. Ask two other customers (not the manager) to read to you what the labels say.

2. Fill your cart only with items that have a picture of the contents on the can or box or whose contents are visible.

3. Call an employment service and ask what jobs are available if you can't read.

4. Use your imagination: Imagine applying for a job and asking the job interviewer to help you fill in the application form. What do you think would happen?

C. You Have Certain Preferences or Necessities

Contact a high school, community college, or university job placement office. Ask for a few minutes to discuss how difficult the following preferences, needs, or conditions would make someone's job search. In spite of what may be legal or not legal, inquire as to whether the following or similar preferences/situations are discussed by career/job counselors when counseling job seekers. The job seeker says:

1. If possible, I would like to not have to work alongside _____.
   (Fill in the blank with any kind of person or population group.)

2. I *must* leave early on Fridays to begin observance of my Sabbath.

3. I have an aging parent whom I must attend to between 3:30 and 4:00 each day,
   or at least every other day.

4. I must take every Tuesday afternoon off for my AIDS treatments.

5. I am wheelchair bound (or have another physical impairment that usually requires certain modifications to my work station).

D. A Different Point of View

Imagine what it would be like to be a foot taller or shorter.

1. How did your perspective of the world change?

2. How did the reaction toward you change?

3. What did people say to you and how did they respond visually?

You will need a group of friends to help you for this. Have the group stand or sit
around you so that passersby cannot see your legs. Try standing on a short stool and
see what kind of reactions you get.

1. How did people respond?

2. What did they say to you?

3. How did they look at you?

4. What did you think was going through their minds?

5. What were your reactions to their reactions?

6. Did you see the world differently?

You might also consider how a person might experience the world from the "short"
perspective. Also consider the difference one's age might make; for example, imagine
you're 4'6" tall and age 9, then age 15.

1. Was the world bigger?

2. Did it look more difficult to negotiate?

3. Were there a number of things you simply couldn't do or were much more difficult to do from this height?

Most of us have wondered about or even wished to be taller (or perhaps shorter) but
have you ever thought of your own reactions to people who are a good deal taller or
shorter than you are?

1. How did you treat them?

2. What were your reactions like?

3. What have your friends said in regard to others who are taller or shorter?

E. What If You Had Another Religion or Had Different Beliefs?

1. Visit the place of worship of several religions. Visit a Buddhist temple, an Islamic mosque, a Jewish temple, a Black church, a Congregational church, a Mexican Catholic church, and an Irish Catholic church if possible. Try to visit during a religious service. Of course, there are many others to visit.

2. Obtain as much information as possible about the religious beliefs and practices. The religious leader will usually be helpful. Which religions have similar beliefs and/or practices? dissimilar?

3. Discuss with family members (or friends who know your religious beliefs) what they would think of your changing your religion.

4. Imagine if you were to marry a person of a different religious faith. What would be the obstacles? How best could the situation be faced?

F. What's in a Home?

The problem of homelessness throughout the world is a well-known fact. The number of issues involved in homelessness are many and quite complex. One of the most vexing, however, may be the way in which homeless people are viewed and related to because of their homelessness. Not all homeless persons look like the stereotyped bag lady or derelict, but once you know a person is homeless how do you and how does society usually react?

1. Visit, or better yet, volunteer for a day of service at a shelter for the homeless. Talk to as many staff and customers as you can.

2. Put on your most miserable/mismatched clothes. Be sure to wear at least two or three coats and shoes that perhaps are too large or do not fit in some way and carry several plastic bags full of items that can be sold or traded. Take a walk through your neighborhood or take a commuter train, a bus ride, or visit a grocery store. Do be careful about this; not everyone likes the homeless.

G. Gender and What It Means

People align themselves on all sides of gender-related issues. We have all been socialized to certain sex roles within our families, cultures, and society. As a result, we may tend to display many behaviors expected of us according to our gender. While most of us accept gender differences to some degree, we are often not aware that both men and women may feel offended by rigid or biased gender expectations. We may not even conceptualize or recognize the frustrations individuals might experience as they perceive how they are being treated by the opposite sex.

1. It is difficult to "put the shoe on the other foot," but perhaps discussions with parents, siblings, or friends can help. If your community has a woman who was the first woman police officer, mayor, and so on, see if you can meet and interview her.

   a. How do men and women perceive or experience the same daily events?

   b. Who is listened to?

   c. Whose opinion is important?

   d. How is one "notified" that he or she is going to be politely tolerated but not listened to?

   e. How do both men and women put into practice such ideas?

   f. Is there a difference in the worldview and style of communicating between the different genders?

2. If you're comfortable enough to risk it, have some friends help you with some cosmetic work. Apply makeup to your hands and face as appropriate to approximate your opposite sex. Use a fake beard or a wig. Dress in slacks or blue jeans and wear a coat to hide your shape. Choose a masculine- or feminine-looking coat as appropriate. Try a bus ride or visit a grocery store to see if reactions to you are different now that you have changed your sex role.

H. What Color Is the Rainbow?

There is ample information that physical characteristics, such as skin color or hair, do influence both perceptions and expectations. Most societies have developed views or notions about what is the "ideal." Information such as a person's features or appearance is scanned, assessed, and reacted to by those around us. What if we were "perfect" or quite "different"? What would our experience be?

1. Again you will need the help of your "makeup-artist" friends. Put on the face, hands, hair, and style of clothing as you so define, or assume the character of either the "ideal" person in this society *or* the characteristics of a person of a cultural identity different from your own. What was your reaction to yourself?

   _____

   _____

   What did your friends think?

   _____

   _____

2. Take a ride on public transportation or visit a grocery store as the "different other." What did you notice during your day?

_____

_____

I. If I Had Only a Little Less Money

No doubt we all might wish for a little more money in our lives. There are always a few more things or better quality things we might wish to buy. Most of us recognize that there are basics to take care of, and once we have taken care of the basics we are left with a little bit of money to spend as we wish. Many of us also have access to money from our friends and family both in times of trouble as well as that little extra for fun. What would happen to our lives or to others' lives if monetary resources simply weren't available? Try the following simulation for a day, then for a week, then for two weeks or a month.

First, in the following chart, make an accounting of what you have.

INCOME FOR THE MONTH (YOUR OWN)	INCOME FROM OTHERS (OR AVAILABLE)	COST OF EACH BASIC (RENT, FOOD, CAR, ETC.)	DISCRETIONARY $ (FOR PLEASURE)
TOTALS			

Then put into practice as many of the following directives as possible. Push yourself.

Directives for One Week

1. Cut out all available discretionary money except $10 ($40 for month).

2. Cut out all money (or purchases for you) from others. If you can't really do this, imagine what you'd have to do if this happened.

3. Cut your food and gasoline purchases by $10 each week ($40 for month).

4. Put all credit cards away if you have them. You're on a cash economy.

5. Give up your automobile for a week or two.

6. Rent no movies since you don't have a VCR. You may keep your TV.

7. When your friends call, tell them you can't go out because you have no money. Don't let them pay for you.

8. Put one-half of all your food stocks away for a week or two. Use only the remainder and what you can purchase on your new budget plan.

9. Unplug your telephone; use only pay phones.

10. Put away three-fourths of your clothes. Do not buy any new clothes.

11. You may spend no more than $8 for any entertainment, including transportation. Remember this comes from a $40 discretionary fund for a month.

12. Spend no more than $3 for a gift for family or friends or make the gift yourself. What were the reactions?

13. Consider what would happen if you could afford only one-half of your heat bill, water bill, electric bill. Call a utility company. Ask them what you could do if you can't pay the bill this month or for the next six months.

14. No bank checks allowed. Cash only.

15. Use no savings: you have none!

16. No laundry or dry cleaning service. Too expensive! (And no one to do it for you!) You can use a laundromat if you wash your clothes yourself.

17. Try out your newfound lifestyle. How "crimped" did it feel? What if this were going to continue for the next six months?

Or, after listing all the things you spend money on each month and the amount you spend, cut that amount by one-fourth then try cutting by one-half. Keep a record of each of the items and note how long it takes to exhaust your available monthly supply of money. Don't forget: list any expenditures not on your original list and remember that money must be deducted from somewhere. What are your trade-offs?

But realize, the true way to experience poorness is to be poor and to know the difference between being poor and having what you now have.

In addition to either of the above simulations, list all the changes you imagine your life would undergo. Some might include:

1. Where do you imagine you would eventually have to live?

2. What kind, if any, of car would you be able to own?

3. How safe would your neighborhood be? How big would your home be?

4. Who would be your neighbors? Who would become your friends?

5. What would happen to old friendships?

6. What would people expect of you?

J. If I Had Only a Little Less Room

The amount and type of physical space we have (or make available to ourselves) for living—our apartment or home—may reflect several factors, such as personal choice, socioeconomic status, age, family needs, cultural ways, and community requirements. The continued growth in the world and U.S. population may affect our choices in the future. Whatever the reasons might be, could you live with or in less physical space?

If you live alone, it won't take much to do the following simulation. If you have a family, it will require cooperation from all—spouse, children, anyone else living with you. Make note not only of how lack of space may structurally affect your living, but also note what effect it may have on social relationships as well as its effect on emotional and psychological stress levels. Note how the more limited space affects immediate home occupants as well as how it affects relationships outside the family.

Note: You will need a lot of masking tape for this project.

1. Imagine that you can only afford about one-half to one-third of the space you now own or rent. Figure out the square footage of your present home and divide by three or two. Can you live in this amount of space? Remember, many do, with more people in the house than you may have currently living with you.

2. Using your masking tape, eliminate whole rooms or portions of rooms in order to get to one-half or one-third of your space. You may keep the hallways just so you can get around!

3. Now, since humans often accumulate things to fill up the space we have available, you have the task of eliminating some of these. Or you can simply move all your furniture into the space left after shrinking your rooms. Use your masking tape wisely. Mark each piece of furniture that can no longer be used because it just doesn't fit anymore. Don't forget: get everyone's agreement on what stays and what goes.

4. If you really want to get realistic, begin taping off one-half of your closet space, cabinets, and refrigerator.

Often an increase in awareness of the totality of our and others' experiences leads to a reassessment of how we might more effectively relate to others. That is, such awarenesses often lead to more understanding in choosing *what* we will do and *how* we will do whatever we do in relationship to others. A greater understanding of this *totality* of human experience is one of the characteristics of a developing multicultural personality. Later, in several activities in Section VII, you are asked to assess your level of multiculturalism. The simulations you completed should have a positive affect on your own growth and development in multiculturalism.

SUMMARY OF SECTION VI
Growth and Development

Now reflect on the information discovered in the foregoing activities. Identify the most critical ideas relevant to:

1. Your self-identity:

2. Your cross-cultural relationships:

3. Expanding your contacts with different others:

4. Suggestions for increasing your multicultural knowledge:

5. List any ideas you should be critically cautious about:

6. Based on your work in Section VI, what message, idea, perception about multiculturalism would you like to share with yourself or your colleagues at this time?

7. List any newly discovered sources from which you could obtain information of a multicultural nature.

SOURCE (book, film, etc.)	NATURE/TYPE OF SOURCE	WHERE TO FIND IT (address, phone, etc.)
1.		
2.		
3.		
4.		
5.		
6.		
7.		
8.		

SECTION

VII

Approaches to Counseling and Counseling Interactions

Background Reading: Chapter 9, "Traditional Approaches to Counseling and Psychotherapy," Chapter 10, "Eclectic and Synergetic Approaches to Counseling and Psychotherapy," and Chapter 11, "The Interaction of Counselor and Client," in John A. Axelson, *Counseling and Development in a Multicultural Society* (3rd ed.). Pacific Grove, Calif.: Brooks/Cole, 1999.

FOR YOUR CONSIDERATION

Given that our educational preparation as a counselor/professional human services worker is essentially a life-long career foundation, consider the following possibilities and questions:

1. If you are 22 to 40 years old, you will likely practice your trade at least until the year 2025–2050.

2. In 2025 the world population will more than double; by 2050 it will likely double again.

3. How will the demographics of the United States likely change in terms of number of people as well as the ethnocultural makeup of the population?

4. How might professional roles and agencies function differently over the next 50 years?

5. How might sociopolitical structures, let alone society-wide values and beliefs and behaviors possibly change, not only in the United States but also around the world?

Counselors and professional helpers in a multicultural society are faced with many exciting yet difficult challenges. One of the first challenges we commonly face is to become cognizant of a number of different theoretical approaches to helping others. Counseling reports and studies suggest that there are at least 130 approaches to counseling and psychotherapy practiced in the United States alone. Most counseling students are exposed to only a fraction of these in their curriculum of study. It is also uncommon for students to be exposed to alternative theories and approaches followed in other countries or within a particular culture, or those practices not considered traditional to the mainstream U.S. culture.

Self-Awareness

Also of major consideration is that, whether novice or expert, both counselors and clients are continuously admonished to "know thyself"—that it is *as critical* to develop a deep awareness of self as it is to know any particular theory or strategy of helping others. Historically, educational exercises to increase our self-awareness have focused on exploring the intrapsychic influences that particular events, beliefs, values, and experiences have upon our own unique individual character or personality.

Social and Cultural Awareness

Beginning during the 1950s and 1960s, however, increased attention was also given to the influence of family *and* society (at large) upon the development of the individual's unique cognitions, beliefs, and behaviors. Since the 1980s and ever increasingly, attention has been paid also to recognizing the power of our own culture and other culturally based influences. It is not just what counselors may value and believe that is of importance, but also what our clients, their families, and their culture may value and believe in, and, most importantly, how they act in accordance with or opposition to these distinctive value and belief systems.

Self as a System

Thus, many counseling and human services education programs have conceptually moved from teaching individual self-awareness to awareness-of-self-in-a-context. We are encouraged to think in terms of self-as-a-part-of, that is, a *system-of-and-with-self,* which necessarily includes family, culture, and society. Today it is believed that to examine the points of intersection and interaction between and within human units is critical in order to discover both shared and divergent beliefs, values, and behaviors.

This consideration of self *as inseparable from relationships with other humans* encourages us to develop awareness and knowledge of those who have differentnesses based on racial, ethnic, or cultural characteristics (or, just as importantly, differentnesses based on gender, condition, status, or preference). From a systemic viewpoint, in order to gain self-awareness and self-knowledge we must necessarily gain awareness and knowledge of such differentnesses. Understanding of the individual self in relationship with others—understanding the complex and constant reciprocal interaction and interinfluencing that occurs between and among humans—is deemed necessary to effectively live in a multicultural society. Behaviors within a family, a culture, a subculture, or between groups and the society as a whole do influence who we are, who we might become, how we think, and how we will act in both the larger and smaller events of life.

The Heritage of Individuality

Still, however expanded this version of self-awareness is, it is usually thought of and practiced in a form and process that is directed to *the advancement of the individual* (whether it be for the counselor or for the client). In large part, that is a heritage of the earliest immigrants and our national form of government in the United States. This encouragement of individuality as exemplified in the Bill of Rights and as addressed in both liberal and conservative movements throughout the history of the United States is an exceptionally important force in our pluralistic nation. This notion of individuality (with its implications) versus such notions as collectivity, "group-ality," internationality, or world oneness (with all their implications) may be at the crux of many cross-cultural issues confronting the deliverer and consumer of human services. In a way, the therapeutic goal of self-actualization (individual potentiation) as well as the actualization of humanity as a whole is confronted in each helping relationship.

In this regard, as helping persons we need to be aware of our potential to influence and impact large segments of the population, possibly even the structure of society. As counselors, as helpers, we generally consider our client unit to be only the individuals we work with; thus, we assist each person and each family to find their solutions to their concerns "one by one by one" or "family by family by family." Most likely we think of the impact we have upon others in rather small figures even when the cumulation of such interventions proves to be exceptionally powerful.

From Individual Health to Community Health

Try to estimate the total number of clients you might influence over the span of your entire career as a counselor. What if in your helping role you worked 48 weeks a year for 30 years and had approximately 28 client contacts a week? This would amount to *40,320 client contacts* in a 30-year period! Even if these contacts might be duplicated with the same client (i.e., every week you see each person twice for 12 weeks) you would still be influencing and impacting directly upon the lives of approximately *10,000 different persons* during your career as a counselor. And if the counseling were a powerful influence in the life of each client, how many people might be influenced by the changes in this single client as he or she returns to family, to work, to society?

Is it possible that a city or state or national law might be approved or disapproved according to the nature of the ideas, beliefs, or values we share with clients during our counseling sessions? If you were a family counselor and saw five families of five persons each and each of these individuals in turn influenced many of the others in their lives, what is the estimate of the number of people you have directly *and* indirectly influenced? Is there a particular bias or value we have and espouse that influences many more persons than we had thought? We may have *enormous* influence upon not only the individual clients and their families but even the fabric of significant portions of the society. And what happens if the persons we individually influence have their own powerful positions of influence beyond their families and their immediate coworkers? If, for example, we influence a group of 25 future juvenile court judges, how might that judicial system become different for hundreds of juveniles, probation workers, attorneys, and law enforcement personnel?

How many different professions of helping are there and how many workers are there within these professions? Estimates of the total number of professionals (master's degree plus) in counseling, social work, psychiatry, psychology, nursing, and related fields range as high as 1 to 1.2 million; estimates for baccalaureate or less prepared midlevel and para-professionals include an additional 1.8 to 2 million persons. The total workforce of human services helpers is estimated to be 2.8 to 3.2 million or approximately 4% to 4.5% of the available labor force. If each of the estimated human services providers saw only 10 individual clients per week, they would together be influencing weekly approximately *30 million* persons (10% of the U.S. population). The size of this potential influence emphasizes the seriousness of our goal of "accessing our awareness and developing our knowledge."

Goals and Responsibilities of the Helping Professions

Helping professions that recognize the importance of such processes as *coparticipation, codetermination, coauthority, coresponsibility, codevelopment,* and *empowerment* are confronted with identifying what the fundamental goals of helping are. Can we conceptualize helping primarily in terms of the individual without considering the social order and the impact the relationships and beliefs that are essential to that individual's life? Can we consider helping to be focused primarily on individuals and their change (behavioral or cognitive) without consideration of the possible reciprocal influences of such change upon the lives of others, upon whole groups, upon large elements of society? Will counselors encourage or even impose only human change that is in accord with their own beliefs or worldview? Will we as counselors be open to changing and challenging our own structures of knowing and operating in the world the same as we encourage others to behave and believe differently than they have? Will we encourage assimilation to a particular cultural template of belief and behavior or accommodation to a pluralism of viewpoints and ways of living? Will we simply *respect* differences and seek tolerance for them, or will we *value*, utilize, and synthesize such differences in order to create new models of growth and development that incorporate different understandings of life and living?

ACTIVITY VII-1
Constructs for Guiding Life and Living

Individuals singly as well as individuals in the company of others develop ideas about what is important in life and the way life should be lived. These ideas are often referred to as concepts or constructs that connote certain understandings, beliefs, or principles of human nature. For example, "individuality" refers to the quality of being an individual. Yet it also refers to the notion that "being an individual" or "acting with individuality" is of some particular *value* to humans. Each of us individually and each cultural group collectively may attach different meanings to an idea or concept shared by many differing human groups. And, since individuals and groups of individuals have different experiences, they also often value and express at different levels and in different ways such shared ideas and concepts about life.

The level of significance we attach to ideas may give an indication of the likelihood of certain behaviors occurring (as opposed to other possible behaviors). However, such concepts are not always in perfect harmony. Thus, living according to these important ideas is not only complex but may create conflicts that must be reconciled within ourselves as well as in relationship to others. In Activity VII-1 we again look at our values toward life and living. These ideas, their meaning and their value, are related to our social growth and development. In a sense, these ideas about humans and human nature are based on past experiences but act as parameters or guidelines in the present experience. And while these life-approach constructs may guide us as we enter into an experience, they often change or are modified as we reassess their usefulness in the face of feedback from that immediate experience.

What we mean is that while certain ideas provide a sense of stability (guidelines) for our approach to ourself and others, applying such ideas is not a static, unchanging phenomenon. The following activity asks you to assess the importance to you of a number of value-related concepts. Which constructs or ideas are compatible or consistent with your own culture or other cultures is a question to be carefully considered. Identifying such ideas and their level of value to you and how they may be different from others' ideas should help in increasing your ability to understand and relate cross-culturally. You may not be sure about the exact definition of some of the constructs listed; nevertheless, based on *your* own understanding of the terms that follow, estimate how valuable each is to you.

Now fill out the following chart. Check each concept as having high importance, moderate importance, or low importance to you or that you have no opinion or do not understand. After you have completed this part of the activity, please respond to the questions that follow.

A. Value Concepts Ranking Chart

HI   = High importance

MI   = Moderate importance

LI   = Low importance

NO   = No opinion

DNU = Do not understand

VALUE CONCEPTS OF LIFE AND LIVING	VALUE TO YOU				
	HI	MI	LI	NO	DNU
1. Aggressiveness/assertiveness					
2. Aging (becoming old)					
3. Authority (accepting)					
4. Behavioral correctness in most situations					
5. Being first/achieving the top					
6. Being liked					
7. Being right (correct)					
8. Being true to self					

VALUE CONCEPTS OF LIFE AND LIVING	VALUE TO YOU				
	HI	MI	LI	NO	DNU
9. Charity/kindness					
10. Collective responsibility					
11. Color of skin					
12. Controlling changes in life					
13. Dependence on others					
14. Education (attaining one's)					
15. Efficiency/concreteness					
16. Employer loyalty to employees					
17. Equality of women with men					
18. Faithful, lasting marriage					
19. Fatherhood					
20. Femininity					
21. Finding answers to problems					
22. Frankness/directness					
23. Free from financial debt					
24. Good health					
25. Gratefulness (saying thanks)					
26. Having clear goals (most always)					
27. Heterosexuality					
28. Hierarchy/structure in families					
29. Honesty/integrity					
30. Honesty/not cheating					
31. Hospitality to guests (show)					
32. Human dignity/worth (all have such)					
33. Independence from others					
34. Individuality/uniqueness					

VALUE CONCEPTS OF LIFE AND LIVING	VALUE TO YOU				
	HI	MI	LI	NO	DNU
35. Inherited property (ownership passed on)					
36. Interethnic marriage (valuing such)					
37. Interracial marriage (valuing such)					
38. Interreligious marriage (valuing such)					
39. Justice/fairness					
40. Karma/fate					
41. Learning (with/out school)					
42. Loyalty to family					
43. Marriage (having one)					
44. Masculinity					
45. Modesty					
46. Money/material resources					
47. Motherhood					
48. Occupation (a certain kind)					
49. Organized religion (should belong to)					
50. Patriotism/active citizenship					
51. Peace/harmony					
52. Political correctness					
53. Preservation of environment					
54. Property ownership (acquiring own)					
55. Psychological problems (having none)					
56. Punctuality/timeliness					
57. Respect for elders/aged					

VALUE CONCEPTS OF LIFE AND LIVING	VALUE TO YOU				
	HI	MI	LI	NO	DNU
58. Respect for youth/children					
59. Sacredness of land/nature					
60. Spirituality (all things have)					
61. Sexual relations					
62. Social status					
63. Welfare assistance (should have)					
64. Work (we should)					
65. Written law (abide by)					

1. List three problems or concerns of living that you currently have (such as job, parents, education).

   Concern 1: _____

   Concern 2: _____

   Concern 3: _____

2. Can you identify concepts from the chart that might relate to the three problems or concerns that you listed in 1 above? Identify the number(s) of the associated concept(s).

   Concern 1: _____ , _____ , _____ , _____, _____ , _____ , _____ , _____

   Concern 2: _____ , _____ , _____ , _____, _____ , _____ , _____ , _____

   Concern 3: _____ , _____ , _____ , _____, _____ , _____ , _____ , _____

3. Are there any concepts that are common to all three concerns? to two concerns? Identify them by number and name.

   Concept Number   Common (Shared) Concepts Associated with My Concerns

   _____   _____

   _____   _____

   _____   _____

4. What is the total number of concepts related to each problem?

   Concern 1: _____ total concepts

   Concern 2: _____ total concepts

   Concern 3: _____ total concepts

5. In each concern, or across all the problem examples, are there concepts that might seem contradictory or in conflict with each other? Identify them by number and name.

_____   _____

_____   _____

_____   _____

6. If the number of concepts related to each concern or problem is large or particularly if there are concepts that seem antithetical to each other, it may be that your underlying value system is complex and/or conflictual; this may make it difficult to take responsibility or to find solutions for the problems or concerns that you identified. On the scale that follows, estimate the complexity level for each of the three concerns/problems.

Complexity Level	Concern 1	Concern 2	Concern 3
Very high			
High			
Moderate			
Low			
Very low			

Note: If the concepts related to any particular problem are quite compatible with each other, then the complexity of finding a solution may be quite low even if the number of concepts is high. Of course, it may still be very difficult to develop a solution.

B. Reviewing Your Value Concepts

1. List your value concepts (by their name) according to how you ranked them on the Value Concepts Ranking Chart.

HIGH IMPORTANCE	MODERATE IMPORTANCE	LOW IMPORTANCE	NO OPINION	DO NOT UNDERSTAND

2. What were your initial impressions of your value concept rankings?

3. Is there apparent consistency or compatibility of the concepts under any of the ranking levels?

4. Are there contradictions within any level? How do you reconcile or explain this?

5. Have another person, preferably someone whose cultural experience or background is different from yours, complete the Value Concepts Ranking Chart.

6. Ask this person to identify three major problems/concerns of life and living that she or he has (or people from a similar culture/background might have).

   Concern 1: _____

   Concern 2: _____

   Concern 3: _____

7. Ask this person to identify the concepts related to each of these concerns/problems as you did in Question A-2.

   Concern 1: _____ , _____ , _____ , _____, _____ , _____ , _____ , _____

   Concern 2: _____ , _____ , _____ , _____, _____ , _____ , _____ , _____

   Concern 3: _____ , _____ , _____ , _____, _____ , _____ , _____ , _____

8. Now have the person list the value concepts according to her/his ranking (on the following chart) as you did for yourself in B-1. What similarities and/or dissimiliarities are there?

HIGH IMPORTANCE	MODERATE IMPORTANCE	LOW IMPORTANCE	NO OPINION	DO NOT UNDERSTAND

Major Similarities   *Major Dissimilarities*

_____   _____

_____   _____

_____   _____

_____   _____

_____   _____

9. Out of all of this exploration, which two or three concepts/ideas do you think are most *central* to how *you* approach life and living? Which two or three concepts/ideas are considered most *central* by your *culturally different* collaborator?

Your Central Concepts   *Other Person's Central Concepts*

1. _____   1. _____

2. _____   2. _____

3. _____   3. _____

C. Value Concepts and the Helping Professions

Now, think about yourself in the role of a counselor, advisor, consultant, friend, or supervisor. You are in a position of influence to other people. Your concepts about life influence whatever advice or suggestions you may give to others. What have you discovered about yourself and/or others in this activity? How might this information be useful to you? In other words, your approach to others is highly influenced by your ideas:

1. About concepts of life and living:

2. About how concepts may be differently valued:

3. About the complex interaction of values and problems:

4. About how concepts might change or how their importance to you might change:

5. About interactions between persons with differing concepts of values:

6. About how knowing all this, you would now try to assist others in addressing their concerns:

ACTIVITY VII-2
Understanding Counseling and Psychotherapy Approaches

Theoretical Constructs

The approaches that are used in counseling and psychotherapy are based on theoretical models that are believed to explain and describe human nature, growth, and development and human problems and the manner in which a person can best be helped. The theoretical models are based on constructs (ideas) that have been logically, clinically, scientifically, and/or experimentally determined and synthesized to form an integrated picture.

Identification of one's own theoretical approach to counseling is an arduous process. You are constantly learning more about yourself as well as different theories of counseling. As such, it may take many years for you to synthesize your awareness, knowledge, and experiences into what may be considered your own theoretical approach. Even then, an approach often combines the ideas and concepts of several theories. Sometimes these different ideas appear to be in conflict or unusual in combination, at least according to a "pure" theory. This exercise will help you review some of the constructs related to major traditional theories of counseling and also assist you in becoming more aware of those constructs with which you most identify or that you believe are most important to you when counseling others.

A. Constructs Found in Traditional Counseling Theories

1. First, go to the following page for the list of 82 items that are related to the traditional theory and practice of counseling. Circle 20 items from this list that are most important to you when counseling others. List them here.

1. _____	11. _____
2. _____	12. _____
3. _____	13. _____
4. _____	14. _____
5. _____	15. _____
6. _____	16. _____
7. _____	17. _____
8. _____	18. _____
9. _____	19. _____
10. _____	20. _____

Selected 82 Items Related to Theory and
Practice of Counseling and Psychotherapy

1. early childhood
2. success/failure identity
3. collective unconscious
4. cognition
5. insight
6. social interest
7. self-perception
8. social personality
9. muscular relaxation
10. empathy
11. social character
12. scientific method
13. interpersonal relations
14. will
15. role playing
16. foreground/background
17. unlimited personal development
18. unconscious
19. value judgments
20. archetypes
21. self-defeating thoughts
22. psychic balance
23. purpose
24. phenomenal field
25. neurotic needs
26. autogenic training
27. genuineness
28. irrational authority
29. external forces
30. dynamisms
31. centering
32. rehearsal
33. mind-body wholeness
34. freedom of choice/responsibility
35. transference/countertransference
36. responsible/irresponsible behavior
37. persona
38. irrational beliefs
39. life/death drives
40. lifestyle
41. conditions of worth

42. flooding
43. unconditional positive regard
44. conformity
45. conditioning
46. self-system
47. subpersonalities
48. simulation
49. body messages
50. human condition
51. psychosexual development
52. commitment
53. anima/animus
54. disputation
55. ego defense mechanisms
56. family constellation
57. congruence
58. reflective listening
59. productive orientation
60. elicited/emitted
61. interpersonal communication
62. contracts
63. how and what
64. being
65. basic drives
66. no punishment
67. shadow
68. homework assignments
69. neurotic anxiety
70. reorientation
71. self-actualization
72. reward/punishment
73. consensual validation
74. assertiveness training
75. here and now
76. nonbeing
77. intrapsychic conflict
78. conscience and guilt
79. self-capacity
80. being-in-the-world
81. character disorder
82. alienation

2. Now list in *order of your own preference* the following three general categories of traditional theories of counseling and psychotherapy: psychodynamic, existential-humanistic, behavioral (i.e., list your first, second, third preference)?

   1st: *behavioral*

   2nd: *existential-humanistic*

   3rd: _____

3. Next, circle which specific subcategories under the psychodynamic, existential-humanistic, and behavioral approaches listed below would *best* identify your preferred orientation to counseling and psychotherapy at this time. (For this and the following "Unscramble" exercise, it may be helpful to go back to the theory reviews in Chapter 9 of *Counseling and Development in a Multicultural Society,* 3rd ed.)

Psychodynamic	*Existential-humanistic*	*Behavioral*
Psychoanalysis	Existential analysis	Conditioned responses
Jung	Rogers	Social learning
Adler	Perls	Ellis
Horney	Assagioli	Glasser
Fromm		
Sullivan		

B. Construct Scramble/Unscramble

Finally, place the "scrambled" 82 construct items under the most appropriate general categories or subcategories of counseling and psychotherapy.

1. Use the form below to place each item under the theory author or theory name that you believe it best goes with or that is most appropriate. The total number of items that fit each category or subcategory is indicated. No item should be used more than once.

2. When you have completed the matching process, check your results with the answers provided.

3. Now that you have noted the suggested placement of the items, go back to the 20 construct items that you selected as important to you in A-1.

   a. Did you identify with any particular theory or theories?

   b. Were there theories for which you selected no items?

   c. Did you discover any surprises or inconsistencies? What does this mean?

82 Items Associated with Theoretical Approach to Counseling and Psychotherapy

Psychoanalytic (13)

1.
2.
3.
4.
5.
6.
7.
8.
9.
10.
11.
12.
13.

Jung (5)
1.
2.
3.
4.
5.

Adler (5)
1.
2.
3.
4.
5.

Horney (2)
1.
2.

Fromm (4)
1.
2.
3.
4.

Sullivan (5)
1.
2.
3.
4.
5.

Existential Analysis (7)
1.
2.
3.
4.
5.
6.
7.

Rogers (10)
1.
2.
3.
4.
5.
6.
7.
8.
9.
10.

Perls (5)
1.
2.
3.
4.
5.

Assagioli (3)
1.
2.
3.

Behavioral (5)
1.
2.
3.
4.
5.

Conditioned Responses (3)
1.
2.
3.

Social Learning (5)
1.
2.
3.
4.
5.

Ellis (5)
1.
2.
3.
4.
5.

Glasser (5)
1.
2.
3.
4.
5.

Answers on next page.

Answers to Construct Scramble/Unscramble

Psychoanalytic
1. early childhood
18. unconscious
35. transference/
countertransference
51. psychosexual
development
65. basic drives
77. intrapsychic conflict
5. insight
22. psychic balance
39. life/death drives
55. ego defense
mechanisms
69. neurotic anxiety
78. conscience and guilt
81. character disorder

Jung
3. collective
unconscious
20. archetypes
37. persona
53. anima/animus
67. shadow

Adler
6. social interest
23. purpose
40. lifestyle
56. family constellation
70. reorientation

Horney
8. social personality
25. neurotic needs

Fromm
11. social character
28. irrational authority
44. conformity
59. productive
orientation

Sullivan
13. interpersonal
relations
30. dynamisms
46. self-system
61. interpersonal
communication
73. consensual validation

Existential Analysis
17. unlimited personal
development
34. freedom of choice/
responsibility
50. human condition
64. being
76. nonbeing
80. being-in-the-world
82. alienation

Rogers
7. self-perception
24. phenomenal field
41. conditions of worth
57. congruence
71. self-actualization
79. self-capacity
10. empathy
27. genuineness
43. unconditional
positive regard
58. reflective listening

Perls
16. foreground/
background
33. mind-body
wholeness
49. body messages
63. how and what
75. here and now

Assagioli
14. will
31. centering
47. subpersonalities

Behavioral
12. scientific method
29. external forces
45. conditioning
60. elicited/emitted
72. reward/punishment

Conditioned Responses
9. muscular relaxation
26. autogenic training
42. flooding

Social Learning
15. role playing
32. rehearsal
48. simulation
62. contracts
74. assertiveness training

Ellis
4. cognition
21. self-defeating
thoughts
38. irrational beliefs
54. disputation
68. homework
assignments

Glasser
2. success/failure
identity
19. value judgments
36. responsible/
irresponsible
behavior
52. commitment
66. no punishment

ACTIVITY VII-3
How Do You Relate to Eclectic and Synergetic Approaches to Counseling and Psychotherapy?

1. Create a list of 10 or more construct items that you believe are important in eclectic and synergetic approaches to counseling and psychotherapy. It may be helpful to review Chapter 10 in *Counseling and Development in a Multicultural Society*, 3rd ed.

   Eclectic   *Synergetic*

   1.   1.

   2.   2.

   3.   3.

   4.   4.

   5.   5.

   6.   6.

   7.   7.

   8.   8.

   9.   9.

   10.   10.

2. What eclectic or synergetic concepts or constructs listed above are most important to you? List three that come to mind.

   Eclectic   *Synergetic*

   1.   1.

   2.   2.

   3.   3.

3. If you have an approach or model that you see as different in some way or form from the traditional, eclectic, or synergetic approaches, identify it and describe it along with its critical ideas and concepts.

   Name of the theory, approach, model, or your own designated title:

Key concepts/items:

1.

2.

3.

4.

5.

4. What have you discovered thus far in this process of identifying your own counseling approach and your own important items of counseling and psychotherapy in the Section VII activities?

5. How would you differentiate (i.e., define) the primary difference(s) between the traditional, eclectic, and synergetic approaches to helping? Indicate the *key characteristics* that would differentiate each from the other two.

    a.   Traditional:

    a.   Eclectic:

    c.   Synergetic:

6. If there are apparent theoretical conflicts or unusual combinations of your approach with any of the traditional, eclectic, or synergetic approaches, explain how you reconcile these differences.

ACTIVITY VII-4
Therapeutic Beliefs and Practices not Indigenous to the Euro-American Culture

In the preceding Section VII activities, the focus has been on counseling and psychotherapy approaches commonly practiced in the United States. These approaches may be characterized as originating from the cultures of the scientific and industrialized Western world. Of course, many other approaches to counseling or healing are practiced around the world and by other cultures. They have developed out of the ways and beliefs of those regions and those groups.

A list of 78 items that are associated with non-Western approaches has been generated for this activity. The items should not be considered stereotypic of non-Western approaches or non-Western cultures; rather the list of items is meant only to suggest that there are many ways to conduct the helping process. The items refer variously to techniques, beliefs, and values that are addressed by non-Western approaches and as related to cultural and/or religious understandings of life. In actual practice, they may be utilized along with Western approaches or alone, according to the counselor or healer's choice. Most items refer to a locally indigenous practiced form of folk medicine but may also be used by Western-educated psychotherapists and counselors practicing in other countries as well as the United States.

Instructions

For this activity you are asked to review the list of 78 items that follows and to indicate your *level of comfort* with each item. Indicate if you have (a) no comfort at all with the item, (b) a possible comfort with considering this kind of item as valid if combined with Western approaches, (c) enough comfort with the item to consider including it *as is* in your own approach to helping.

To give an example of the breadth of the items, consider that they have been drawn from the practices and beliefs within ethnocultural groups such as:

Navajo	Polish	German
Gypsy	British	Jewish
Swedish	Japanese	Brazilian
Italian	Mexican	Jamaican
Hindu	Iranian	Yoruban
Nepalese	Russian	Greek
Zulu	Appalachian	Irish
Norwegian	Portuguese	French Canadian

From racial/ethnic groups:

Asian	Hispanic	European
African	Native American	Semitic

According to religious groups and spiritual practices:

Hinduism	Islamism	Jewish
Buddhism	Voodooism	Christian

Many of the following 78 items may be thought to be primitive and/or archaic according to standard Western-scientific approaches to helping. Nevertheless, they comprise activities that occur in therapeutic endeavors to help people resolve life difficulties even today. They may be held as absolutes; that is, they may be understood as totally appropriate and approved activities of healing and helping by both helper and helpee, although it is unlikely any of the items are practiced throughout the entire culture.

Comfort Level List of Items

Key: Column A = No comfort at all (can't use or don't understand)

Column B = Possible comfort (if combined with Western approaches)

Column C = Some comfort with using as is

SELECTED ITEMS FROM AROUND THE WORLD	COMFORT LEVEL WITH ITEM		
	A NO COMFORT	B POSSIBLE COMFORT	C SOME COMFORT
1. Physically inducing visions	✓		✗
2. Drug-inducing visions	✓		
3. Worshiping family ancestors		✓	
4. Spirit possession (appeasing them)	✓		
5. Worshiping natural forces		✓	
6. Reincarnation		✓	
7. Animal/food sacrifice		✓	
8. Joss/fate (accept as it is)		✓	
9. Trances		✓	
10. Singing marathons			✓
11. Sand painting			✓
12. Bury person in the earth	✓		
13. Use multiple dimensions of time		✓	
14. Submission is a virtue		✓	
15. Chants to spirits		✓	
16. Use of mediums/psychics		✓	
17. Life is not controllable			✓
18. Use of herbs/potions		✓	
19. Extinguish emotion		✓	
20. Caste/place is inherited/accept it		✓	
21. Be healed by becoming healer		✓	
22. Exorcism ceremonies	✓		

| | COMFORT LEVEL WITH ITEM | | |
SELECTED ITEMS FROM AROUND THE WORLD	A NO COMFORT	B POSSIBLE COMFORT	C SOME COMFORT
23. Use of witchcraft/magic		✓	
24. Painting one's body			✓
25. "Reading" bones/charms		✓	
26. Creating secret names			✓
27. Inducing physical pain	✓		
28. One's plight a community affair		✓	
29. Life is misery (look to the "next")		✓	
30. Belief in existence of evil		✓	
31. Isolation of self from others	✓		
32. Use of sweat lodge		✓	
33. Use of regression		✓	
34. Thought reform (brainwashing)	✓		
35. Dreams give direction (allow them to)			✓
36. Vision-quests			✓
37. Wearing of masks, animal skins			✓
38. Uphold/accept tradition rigidly			✓
39. Induce physical exhaustion	✓		
40. Medication is answer to everything		✓	
41. Trust no one	✓		
42. Humans are powerless	✓		
43. Mutual obligation to other must be observed (beyond reason)		✓	
44. One never suffers enough	✓		
45. Use of snakes in healing rituals		✓	

SELECTED ITEMS FROM AROUND THE WORLD	COMFORT LEVEL WITH ITEM		
	A NO COMFORT	B POSSIBLE COMFORT	C SOME COMFORT
46. Fasting to point of weakness		✓	
47. Self-condemnation encouraged		✓	
48. Self-mutilation encouraged	✓		
49. Filial piety at all cost	✓		
50. Absolute reverence of aged		✓	
51. Blood-letting ("leeching")	✓		
52. Ice baths/hot baths			✓
53. Use of magic/illusion			✓
54. Use of "frenzied" parties/feasting			✓
55. Encourage verbal hostility	✓		
56. Prescribe rigid gender roles	✓		
57. Prescribe exhausting physical activity (running, swimming, . . .)		✓	
58. Use of costumes and ceremony			✓
59. Use of "cleansing" rituals			✓
60. Wear sacred amulets/charms			✓
61. Encourage overeating		✓	
62. Give child to another family	✓		
63. Eating specific animal parts (e.g., genitals)	✓		
64. Communicate with family head only (not client)		✓	
65. Valuing totems		✓	
66. Use of rituals to ward off evil eye/evil spirits	✓		
67. Building monuments, sculptures			✓

SELECTED ITEMS FROM AROUND THE WORLD	COMFORT LEVEL WITH ITEM		
	A NO COMFORT	B POSSIBLE COMFORT	C SOME COMFORT
68. Lying for one's own good		✓	
69. Punishment of child/spouse		✓	
70. Accept suicide as honorable		✓	
71. Wailing to rid grief			✓
72. Trading wealth for status/ wife/self-esteem		✓	
73. "Burying" oneself in work		✓	
74. Therapists/healers are only guests, not experts		✓	
75. Feelings should never be revealed		✓	
76. Therapy is a process of bartering abilities (e.g., this for that)	✓		
77. *Only* the future counts		✓	
78. Sharing burdens is bad		✓	

1. List the 78 items according to the comfort level category you assigned to them.

   a. Category A—No comfort at all; couldn't utilize:

   b. Category B—Possibly use combined with traditional Western approaches:

   c. Category C—Comfort with using technique or idea "as is":

2. In general, what is it about any item or grouping of items that makes it possible or impossible to consider its use as an intervention strategy or to accept it as a belief that guides behavior?

3. What if your client believed in or asked you to prescribe or assist in one of the "no comfort at all; couldn't utilize" items? How would you handle this? What would be your rationale? How might you keep the counselor/client relationship healthy?

4. Are there items that if you rephrased them or if they had different wording would appear to be similar to Western ideas or techniques or approaches to counseling and therapy? List a few and restate in Western-scientific terms.

	Item	*Western Restatement*
1.		
2.		
3.		
4.		
5.		
6.		
7.		
8.		
9.		
10.		

5. Several of these non-Western items often seem to provide relief of human problems or concerns. What do you think is the reason or explanation for this success? Is there a common theme or idea that seems to underlie these non-Western items?

ACTIVITY VII-5
Exploring Ethical Issues and Standards

Consider the following questions. Small group discussion with participants of other cultures is highly recommended. Consider each question and record the differing answers.

A. Professional Helper's Responsibility

1. Is your responsibility to the welfare of your client, to family members, to the agency with which you work, to society, or to your own perceptions?

2. When should you refer a client to another professional or agency?

3. If you refer, when is your responsibility ended?

4. What is the client's responsibility in the helping process? Do you have a responsibility to inform the client of his or her responsibility? Explain.

5. Is it your responsibility to know about the client's cultural background, critical beliefs, values, and cultural experiences? Explain.

6. Is it your responsibility to incorporate beliefs and practices of the client's culture into the helping process? Explain.

B. Client/Helper Relationship

1. Should you inform a client of the nature of the therapeutic relationship that you want to establish? The kind of techniques you use? Explain.

2. Should you tell your client your philosophy of helping? Why or why not?

3. If your employing agency has policies regarding the disposition of certain information, should you tell your client (e.g., pregnancy, abortion, cheating)? Should you confront the policies of your agency if they do not follow (or if they exaggerate) the Family Privacy Act?

4. What should you do if certain topics are taboo according to the client's culture?

5. Should you openly discuss your values or beliefs concerning any topic (e.g., equality in marriage, child rearing practices)? Explain.

6. Should clients who are culturally deviant (from mainstream standards) be encouraged to conform? Why or why not?

C. Confidentiality

1. Should information given in confidence be revealed when there is clear danger to the client or society? (*Tarasoff* v. *Board of Regents of the University of California,* 1969, although not decisive in all states is a useful reference.)

2. If there is no clear danger to client or society, yet a client's cultural practice or tradition is a violation of the law, should you report it (e.g., "stealing" young girls of the same ethnic group for marriage to others within that group or insisting that 13-year-olds get married)?

3. If a child client is of a culture that believes all problems should be discussed first with the head of the household, what should you do? What if you know the child would be ostracized or cast out of the family for violating the cultural norms?

4. How should you handle parents' inquiries regarding problems discussed in the interview?

5. Can you mention clients' names in conferences with others? Should you mention their cultural beliefs or values?

D. Professional Helper Values

1. Should you make your values clear to your clients? How would you do this?

2. To what degree *should* your values enter into the relationship?

3. Is it possible to do "value-free" human services work? Explain.

4. What basic set of values do you think is essential to communicate in a therapeutic relationship?

5. Should counseling be an effort whereby the client is helped to develop/learn correct behavior in order to have less conflict with the rest of society?

E. The Professional's Personality and Needs

1. Can a professional exclude her or his needs and personality from the helping relationship? Explain.

2. Are the helper's own mental health, self-integration, and self-awareness important? Explain.

3. How do personal needs affect the helping relationship (as a hindrance or an asset)?

Selected Needs of Professional Helpers

- To have control and power
- To change others in the direction of your values
- To be nurturing and helpful
- To feel important, adequate, and respected
- To be appreciated and recognized by others
- To be confirmed as a competent counselor
- To be productive and attain recognition

4. Rank order the above needs for yourself; 1 = most important, 2 = next most important, and so on.

5. Given all your cultural explorations to this point and your previous rank ordering of selected needs, are there clients of diverse backgrounds who you feel would be very difficult for you to work with? Identify them and what might be the major difficulty.

    Culture Background
    (or Type of Person)   *Major Difficulty*

    a. _____   _____

    b. _____   _____

    c. _____   _____

F. Other Possible Activities

1. Survey human services providers in various settings (schools, mental health agency, family agency, etc.). Ask them to rank order from a list of theoretical orientations compiled by you the counseling approaches toward which they believe they lean. (Refer to Activities VII-2, VII-3, and VII-4.)

2. Develop a profile of what you believe would be an effective multicultural counselor.

3. Write a code of ethics that would be appropriate for a multicultural counselor.

ACTIVITY VII-6
Cultural Awareness in Providing Human Services

The appropriateness of a professional's clinical judgment is important since the direction of client treatment depends on it. Most counselors and human services providers take into account a client's background of cultural experiences and why and how that information might call for a different judgment than would be made otherwise.

Taking into consideration the role that culture can play in mental health is also of major importance. However, supposed cultural differences used in making diagnostic judgments often have little research support. Even if a pattern of behavior is believed to be common for members of an ethnic/racial group, it may still indicate a mental health condition or, on occasion, serious pathology. Thus, it is important not to mistake a serious disorder for culturally normal behavior and, of course, not to judge culturally normal behavior as a disorder. For example, consider the following five hypothetical illustrations:

1. A Black woman from the South (United States) reports feelings of persecution.

2. A White woman living in New England reports feelings of persecution.

3. A Native American man experiences distress when refusing to join his coworkers for drinks every Friday night.

4. A Western-educated Iranian has great difficulty accepting his American wife's "show of independence" whenever his parents visit from Iran.

5. An Irish heritage male (third generation) believes it is better, certainly more appropriate, to "just let things blow over" rather than argue with his spouse.

Using whatever information or considerations you have at hand, would you take into account the above cultural backgrounds? If so, what would be important in each of the above situations?

List some examples where you believe helpers should be sensitive to the role that culture might play in mental health conditions and in making appropriate clinical judgments.

ACTIVITY VII-7
Cultural Applications in Providing Human Services

Although valid research literature on cultural differences is expanding, you still will have to draw upon the experiences of your professional colleagues, your clients' families, and the clients themselves in deciding what is usual or unusual, normal or abnormal for members of racial/ethnic groups and other identified cultural/population groups such as the disabled, the elderly, and gays or lesbians. You may also have to innovate creative therapeutic approaches and interventions to meet special conditions.

For example, it is customary in cases of posttraumatic stress disorder to encourage the client to talk openly about the traumatic event and to freely express emotions (catharsis). *However,* it has been found that for Cambodian refugees in the United States to talk about their wartime experiences often makes their symptoms worse and reactivates old fears. Some of the predominant signs are sleeplessness, inability to concentrate, nightmares, disturbing thoughts, and fear of loud noises or of attachment to others.

How might you explain the lack of therapeutic progress in this situation?

1. On the basis of cultural background:

2. On the basis of traditional (Western) approaches to counseling and human services work:

A PERSPECTIVE FOR YOUR FURTHER CONSIDERATION

Traditional Cambodians and other Asian populations believe that personal bad fortune may arise from dishonorable events in a previous life or in events in history of the nation and, as a result, shame must be experienced by the person or on behalf of the entire nation.

Here are some implications and directions for your consideration in this example of Cambodian beliefs. Read carefully the following hypotheses:

1. The use of individual catharsis as a standard therapeutic procedure is blocked by avoidance behavior that is unknowingly produced by the client as a defense against intense feelings of shame.

2. Traditional group counseling or group therapy aimed at sharing of traumatic experiences and acceptance of each other's emotional pain is not likely to be effective because the group members are all locked into the same collective avoidance behavior produced by the intense feelings of shame.

3. Clinical experiences with posttraumatic stress generally indicate that early intervention is important to prevent a chronic condition of the disorder, thus resolution of the stress is necessary and this situation cannot be viewed as favorable.

4. The stress symptoms are signs of other personal or emotional problems and are not related to traumatic events from the Cambodian wartime experience.

5. Shame, guilt, and blame all fall within the same general category of negative feelings or emotions; however, it is the underlying cultural beliefs that produce these negative feelings and thus must be challenged and questioned until the belief no longer produces the negative symptoms and painful feelings.

6. Is shame a revered cultural belief held by many Cambodians and other Asians? If so, it is important to talk about this belief and the implications that it has for life and one's mental and emotional health.

7. Is it unethical counselor behavior to influence, alter, or tamper with long-enduring Cambodian belief systems? If so, perhaps this situation cannot be resolved according to traditional (Western) counseling approaches.

What are your reactions to the above hypotheses?

Which hypotheses seem most relevant and feasible to you?

Would you add other hypotheses or considerations?

What one personal awareness stands out the most for you as a result of this activity?

SUMMARY OF SECTION VII
Approaches to Counseling and Counseling Interactions

Now reflect on the information discovered in the this section. Identify the most critical ideas relevant to:

1. Your self-identity:

2. Your cross-cultural relationships:

3. Expanding your contacts with different others:

4. Suggestions for increasing your multicultural knowledge:

5. List ideas about which you should be critically cautious:

6. Based on your work in Section VII, what message, idea, perception about multiculturalism would you like to share with yourself or your colleagues at this time?

7. List any newly discovered sources from which you could obtain information of a multicultural nature.

SOURCE (book, film, etc.)	NATURE/TYPE OF SOURCE	WHERE TO FIND IT (address, phone, etc.)
1.		
2.		
3.		
4.		
5.		
6.		
7.		
8.		

VIII

Multiculturalism as a Force and Influence in Human Relationships

Background Reading: Chapters 1 through 11 in John A. Axelson, *Counseling and Development in a Multicultural Society* (3rd ed.). Pacific Grove, Calif.: Brooks/Cole, 1999.

FOR YOUR CONSIDERATION

As noted previously, worldwide population projections as well as potential changes in ethnocultural demographics in the United States (and elsewhere) suggest that counselors and human services professional will be challenged by an increasing array of diverse culture-based belief systems. For example, as voter demographics change, given the growth of "nonmajority" populations, many communities (perhaps the nation as well) will likely experience changes, in a multitude of laws and regulatory mechanisms. If elements of the fabric of this society undergo major modification (or evolution), what "American" beliefs and norms might most be a issue? What traditional U.S. values might most be challenged? What sociopolitical role might counselors play in such processes, both as social advocates within the society as a whole and within the client-counselor helping relationship?

Such potential changes encourage us to review the history of the United States. In spite of several obvious difficulties in cross-cultural relationships, this history is redundant with the incorporation of differing heritage groups right up to the present. Overall, its seems that the United States has been successful at this task. We need to ensure that the role human services professionals play will help promote a "healthy" national environment that will nourish the continued growth and development of all its peoples.

Cultural Connectedness

We all live in a changing world filled with diverse influences and lifestyles. We are increasingly exposed to a variety of changing styles and approaches to life and living. We may appreciate some of these ways of being even if we do not understand them; and some we may understand but find difficult to appreciate or tolerate. Nevertheless, the world we and future generations will live in increasingly demands that we develop abilities to live harmoniously with others. From unique individual diversities and situations to biracial and bicultural marriages to economic system interdependence, we are all increasingly connected to others.

Of course, connections among peoples have always existed but these are more frequent and appear to have greater impact on all of us today. Over the past decade, world events indicate that the eras of colonization and domination by any one group or nation over any other group or nation may be coming to a close. This is occurring even as we recognize the tragic eruptions of tensions and conflicts between newly forming and reforming nations. Without question, the United States and Russia are the most pluralistic nations in the world.

The United States is fortunate to be among the most pluralistic *and* developed nations in the world. As such it is in a key position to foster the development and growth of the concept of multiculturalism as a positive force in worldwide development. You might reflect on the following questions:

1. Is multiculturalism necessary as a viewpoint and as a direction? Does it offer a promise for the future? What are its disadvantages?

2. How might you and others promote multicultural connectedness?

3. What multicultural understandings or abilities do you believe you possess?

4. What is the nature (level) of your commitment to participate in fostering multiculturalism? Give an example of how you do or can demonstrate your concern.

As professionals and as citizens of this nation, we know that developing multicultural understandings—of ourselves, of different others, of interactional relationships, of theoretical and practical concepts that explain human relationships and our potential influence upon such relationships—is a complex and profoundly important endeavor. We are asked to demonstrate the highest level of human sensitivity and concern. We are asked to integrate and synthesize an enormous array of information and levels of awareness and knowledge. An appreciation of multiculturalism also asks us to continuously examine and reexamine our values, beliefs, and behaviors. It asks us to become aware of both useful and not so useful ways of thinking as taught, reinforced, and reaffirmed over our life span. As possible agents of change and promoters of multiculturalism, we are often expected to "see beyond" that which we can presently observe, which may limit potentiation, in order to imagine new possibilities that address the potentials of the human character and human nature.

In summary, we are all confronted and challenged as citizens and human services professionals to make a consistent and constant effort to develop a comprehensive foundation of knowledge about self, about different others, and about our professions. We are asked to encourage human connectedness by developing awareness and knowledge of the many purposes and manners of living in families, cultures, and societies. Accessing and synthesizing this diverse information and awareness into forms of knowledge, allows us to develop the skills necessary to five effectively as well as encourage effective living in a multicultural society.

The activities in this section ask you to examine your cultural connectedness with yourself and with others.

Developing your sense of awareness and discovering your own cultural identities might seem to be very complex tasks. This is because most of us have multiple identities about which we may not be fully aware. As an example, an individual could identify—on different levels of importance—with German ethnics, the elderly and retired, the divorced, and with companions who live in rural communities. The concept of diversity most simply recognizes the existence of multiple manners and conditions of life and living. In the following activities, you will be asked to examine the identities you have discovered in yourself and to consider how this information can be an asset to you as a person and in your work as a helper. Although identities such as racial, ethnic, socioeconomic, occupational, and religious may be the most obvious or important to you, you can also investigate other cultural facets of yourself and your relationships with people who are similar or dissimilar to you.

Activity VIII-1
Bicultural Identification

For this exercise's purpose, bicultural identification basically addresses our relationship between a "dominant society's" set of beliefs and norms and the set of beliefs and norms of our own culture. Essentially, we might be acculturated to act in ways that are in accord with both, one or the other, or neither cultural unit.

1. Describe what you think persons with the given identities below would be like (personal characteristics, politics, beliefs, behaviors, family structure, work values). Consider how persons with such identities fit into a "dominant societal culture." How might each experience life differently?

   a. Bicultural identity.

   b. Acculturated to dominant societal themes.

   c. Acculturated to persons's own culture.

   d. Acculturated to neither dominant or own.

2. How would you position yourself in regard to your acculturation to the dominant societal culture and to your own? Circle your position accordingly on the chart below; that is, is your acculturation high or low in relation to the dominant societal culture? High or low in regard to your own cultural identification? What is your identity status?

ACCULTURATED TO DOMINANT SOCIETAL CULTURAL UNIT	ACCULTURATED TO YOUR OWN CULTURAL GROUP UNIT
High	High
Moderate	Moderate
Low	Low

a. Compare your level of acculturation in both cultural units. What does acculturation to one, both, or no aspect of society or cultural heritage mean in your life and living?

b. How would you identify yourself? Primarily acculturated to dominant societal themes? Primarily acculturated to the themes of your own cultural heritage? Moderately acculturated to both? Marginally (minimally) acculturated to either? How do you feel about this identity?

c. Is or can this nature of acculturation to either or both cultural units be problematic for you? for others? Explain.

d. Did you assign yourself correctly *but* want to be different? Explain how you might achieve a different personal identity status.

e. Would a rank position of "moderate and moderate" be more accurate? What words would you use to identify a person who is moderately acculturated to both the dominant society and to his or her own culture?

f. Do you think it really is or is not important to be bicultural? How would it help your life? How would it hurt your life?

3. Identify at least two reasons why it can be valuable to be predominantly acculturated to one particular group in a multicultural society.

a.

b.

4. Identify two possible difficulties persons predominantly acculturated to one particular group might experience in relation to the rest of society.

a.

b.

5. Identify at least two reasons why it can be valuable to be acculturated to the dominant themes in a multicultural society.

a.

b.

6. Identify two possible difficulties of being acculturated to the dominant themes of society, even a multicultural one.

a.

b.

ACTIVITY VIII-2
Subcultural Identification

We may belong to a variety of different subgroups or categories of being in this society. These subgroups are organized around some shared commonality. For a subgroup to have subcultural importance in our life and living basically means that this group has values, beliefs, behaviors, and viewpoints associated with it that we approve of or that we are highly influenced by. Membership may be a result of choice or status or both. Membership may, among other reasons, be related to age; sex; income; physical, emotional, or medical issues; needs; interests; beliefs; experiences; or societal culture. Some examples include self-help groups, professional organizations, gangs, unique peer groups, youth, the poor, people in recovery, the elderly, disabled persons, religious groups, or political groups. Sometimes our membership in such groups can lead to negative experiences with others, simply because of our affiliation. And subcultural group members also demonstrate a range of diversity among themselves. For example, people in AA come from many different ethnic, racial, and economic groups.

Subcultural groups that we identify with (or belong to) have extremely powerful influences on our thoughts, behaviors, and beliefs. Their influence may be more powerful than our membership status in other groups within the society. As noted, membership alone may powerfully influence others' perception of us and prompt how they act toward us. We suggest you create a chart of your own subcultural group memberships as described below.

1. In column one, identify the subgroups that you belong to. You may want to discuss this with some others to generate possible categories of such subcultural groups.

2. In column two, estimate the power of influence each subgroup has in your life or that powerfully influences others' perceptions or treatment of you (10 = very powerful influence, 5 = moderate influence, 0 = very little influence).

3. In column three, identify whether you feel positive (+) or negative (–) about your membership; that is, whether you're glad or not glad to be part of this subgroup.

4. In column four, identify whether or not your membership in this group is

   A = not a problem to you nor to others; B = not a problem to you but is a problem to others; C = is a problem to you as well as to others; or D = is a problem to you but not to others.

Subculture Memberships	Power of Influence of Your Membership		Postive/Negative Feeling about Membership	Nature of Being a Problem
	Upon Self	Upon Others		
1. _____	_____	_____	_____	_____
2. _____	_____	_____	_____	_____
3. _____	_____	_____	_____	_____
4. _____	_____	_____	_____	_____
5. _____	_____	_____	_____	_____
6. _____	_____	_____	_____	_____
7. _____	_____	_____	_____	_____
8. _____	_____	_____	_____	_____
9. _____	_____	_____	_____	_____
10. _____	_____	_____	_____	_____

5. Circle the two subcultural groups you identified that are most influential in your life either in terms of what they mean to you or because of what your membership may mean to others. Explain how this may be positive or negative for you.

6. Name the most significant values or norms promulgated by the two most influential subculture groups to which you belong.

7. Do any of your subcultural group memberships predominate in your life—that is, have *the most* powerful influence regardless of your other group memberships? What kind of problems does this pose for you:

   a. In terms of your own self-concept/self-identity?

   b. Within your family?

   c. Within your peer/friendship circles?

   d. Within your racial/ethnic cultural heritage grouping?

   e. With other cultural groups?

   f. In the dominant society at large?

   g. In your work (now or in the future) as a counselor?

ACTIVITY VIII-3
Multicultural Identification

Bicultural identification basically involves our relationship with and between the dominant society and our own culture. We might act in accord with both, one or the other, or neither cultural unit. Subcultural identification may play a powerful role in influencing our interactions with others as well as our concept of self. Multicultural identification introduces another but more comprehensive idea of conceptualizing our position vis-à-vis the human groupings that make up a society. In the "Introduction" to this manual, it was suggested that the multicultural personality is one that can be defined as being able to relate to and value a multitude of cultural and subcultural groups. Multiculturalism, as such, refers to our ability to appreciate individuals and groups that are subtly or significantly different from us. It asks that we understand and accept as valuable, viewpoints and behaviors that may be quite different from our own. It also asks that we develop awareness and understanding of our own cultural heritage.

Multiculturalism as a theoretical perspective or *posture of valuing others of differentness* further asks that we try to understand others from their perspective *even* when there are apparently few points of agreement in values or behaviors. It challenges us to develop ways of living harmoniously with others in the face of such differences. As examples, consider that some cultures seem orientated toward a posture of openness to others. Some cultures act as if they were "walking a tightrope" between their own and another culture. Some seem orientated to forcing or imposing their values and behaviors on all the rest (making "them" just like "us").

As we know, the world is becoming increasingly complex. Nations and peoples are recognizing that they are more systemically interdependent than ever before. Population growth and national and societal changes reemphasize the need to develop harmonious relationships between and among the multitude of cultures and subcultures. The greater our sense of multiculturalism—that is, the more we develop a multicultural personality—the more we will be able to meet the demands of a changing world.

1. Given this idea of multiculturalism, rank yourself high or low in regard to identifying with or relating to the following example groups. High = strong identification with/ability to relate to this human grouping. Low = low identification with/ability to relate to this human grouping.

   Note: A moderate affiliation is also possible, but you are asked to consider this later. Also note that the subcultural category includes five examples of subgroups. You can substitute some other subcultural group, but do not numerically add more subgroups to the list.

   Subgroup #1 = Physically disabled persons
   Subgroup #2 = Recovering (formerly addicted) persons
   Subgroup #3 = Homosexual persons
   Subgroup #4 = Persons of the opposite sex—identify as M or F
   Subgroup #5 = Underclass poor

2. Identify substitutions for any subgroup above.

#	Removed	Substitution
____	_____	_____
____	_____	_____
____	_____	_____

   Also make this substitution in question 3 and on the following ranking chart.

3. If the highest score on multiculturalism is 120 points, and the lowest possible score is 10 points, what would be your guess as to your multiculturalism point total? My guess is _____ points.

   What is your own cultural background or identification?

Rank yourself high or low regarding your ability to identify with each of the human groupings below.

Society at large	_____
European American	_____
African American	_____
Asian American	_____
Hispanic American	_____
Native American	_____
Middle Eastern American	_____
Subcultures	
#1 Physically disabled	_____
#2 Recovering	_____
#3 Homosexual	_____
#4 Opposite sex	_____
#5 Underclass poor	_____

Total number of high rankings equals	_____

4. Each high answer is worth 10 points; low = 0 points. Count the number of high answers and multiply by 10. How many points did you earn on this ranking scale? Your actual number of multiculturalism points is _____.

Information Note: In the two-option ranking (high or low scheme) there are 4096 *permutations* (arrangements) possible including the "all high" or "all low" ranking arrangement. Given the large number of statistical arrangements possible, there is great variability even within a grouping of scores. For example, there are around 2700 arrangements for arriving at a score in the 50s, 60s, or 70s. A normal bell-shaped curve of the statistical distribution of scores indicates that most of us would cluster around a score in the 50s, 60s, or 70s. See the next information box for additional information.*

*Calculations provided with the assistance of Dr. George Litton, National-Louis University.

5. Possible multicultural rankings, high, moderate, low.

As indicated in the information box above, a large number of possible "identify with/relate to" ranking combinations exist. On the following chart use a ranking scale of high, moderate, or low in estimating your multiculturalism. Use of the moderate rank rather than just high or low obviously increases the possibilities. You may feel this allows you to rank yourself more accurately (fairly).

Columns 1 through 4 and 11 show possible sample arrangements. Column 1 shows the theoretical "all high" position. Column 11 shows the theoretical "all low" position. Columns 2, 3 and 4 show sample possibilities of ranking combinations.

a. Now use column 5 to rank yourself in relation to each of the selected groups; that is, rank how you relate to each of the groups identified in the left-hand column.

b. Use column 6 to have someone from your family rank herself or himself in terms of her or his relating to each of these groups.

c. Use column 7 to have another person (nonfamily) of your culture rank him/herself in similar fashion.

d. Use columns 8, 9, and 10 to have three persons from another culture or subculture group rank themselves. Note: You may prefer to choose three different persons from the same culture or one person from each of three different cultures. Keep a record of their cultural heritage.

Now we can again hypothetically rank ourselves on multicultural points: high = 10 points, mod = 6 points, and low = 1 point. We can assume that higher point totals mean one is "higher" on multiculturalism; that is, a higher score suggests that we might identify with and/or can relate well with many different kinds of people. This kind of personality would be more rather than less helpful in a pluralistic society. On the following chart the scores for the hypothetical arrangements are: Column 1, the most multicultural personality, would be 10 points × 12 = 120. Column 2, the least multicultural personality, would be 1 point × 12 = 12. Columns 2, 3, and 4 represent just a few of the possibilities of ranking/scoring.

Column 2 = 59 points
Column 3 = 40 points
Column 4 = 86 points

Information Note: In the three-option ranking, there are 531,444 permutations (arrangements) including the "all high" and "all low" possibilities.* In other words, we might basically score somewhat highly on multicultural "points" yet still have a particular cultural or subcultural group we do not relate highly (or even moderately) toward (see column 4). We might also score low on multicultural points yet relate highly to a particular cultural/subcultural group (see column 3). Given the arrangements possible, a normal statistical distribution of scores indicates that most of us would cluster around the 50s, 60s, or 70s. But we do not yet have research indicating what *is* a normal distribution in the United States.

---

*Calculations provided with the assistance of Dr. George Litton, National-Louis University.

RANKING CHART

	1	2	3	4	5	6	7	8	9	10	11
Society at large	high	low	high	high							low
European American	high	mod	low	high							low
African American	high	mod	low	mod							low
Asian American	high	high	low	mod							low
Hispanic American	high	mod	high	low							low
Native American	high	mod	mod	high							low
Middle Eastern American	high	low	low	mod							low
SC #1 Physically disabled	high	low	low	high							low
SC #2 Recovering	high	high	low	high							low
SC #3 Homosexual	high	low	low	high							low
SC #4 Opposite sex (M/F)	high	high	low	low							low
Sc #5 Underclass poor	high	low	mod	mod							low

6. Where do you fall on the scales of multiculturalism?

   a. Your multicultural rating score (col. 5) is   _____

   b. Your family member's score of multiculturalism (col. 6) is   _____

   c. Another member of your culture's score (col. 7) is   _____

   d. Person A from different group (col. 8):   _____

   e. Person B from different group (col. 9):   _____

   f. Person C from different group (col. 10):   _____

   g. What do the scores suggest to you? Were you surprised by any scores?

      (1) Did the other family member score as you anticipated or expected?

      (2) Did the other person (nonfamily) of your culture score as you anticipated or expected?

      (3) Did the members of another culture score as you anticipated or expected?

7. Are there "sets of groupings" you relate high or low to? Identify:

   _____ , _____ , _____ .

8. How does the average score of your three-person cultural grouping compare to the three-person grouping from a different culture?

9. a. What similarities/dissimilarities exist between your grouping and the different groupings?

   b. How might this be useful information if you were counseling someone from this other culture?

10. What group or set of groups do you moderately identify with/relate to? Identify:

   _____ , _____ , _____ ,

   _____ .

11. How similar are your rankings/scores to what you originally estimated your level of multiculturalism to be?

   a. Estimated points in Question 1: _____ .

   b. Your actual point total from column 5 above: _____ .

12. What does this information mean to you? Remember, this is not a sophisticated instrument and your rank/score does not in any way define your multiculturalism status. This simply is an exercise to prompt our awareness. Nevertheless:

a. Is your self-determined identification with any culture grouping (or set of cultural groupings) of significance relative to the way you act toward others?

   In general _____. How so?

   In a specific instance _____. How so?

b. Do you think that your self-determined identification with any particular group *when known to others* influences the way others act toward you?

   In general _____. How so?

   In a specific instance _____. How so?

c. How is the data you generated meaningful to you? How might it prove to be of advantage/disadvantage to you in this changing world?

d. How useful (to you) are the rankings/scorings that others gave to themselves, (i.e., useful to you for the purpose of understanding others)?

13. What areas of cultural understanding would you now work on? What actions or activities could you undertake to change a moderate or low score to a high score?

   Area to Work On   *Action to Undertake*

a. _____   _____

                                  _____

                                  _____

                                  _____

b. _____   _____

                                  _____

                                  _____

                                  _____

14. If you were to undertake to improve on your ability to relate to any particular group (grouping), can you foresee any difficulty or changes in your ability to relate to any *other* group to which you currently relate highly? Identify:

   a. Possible difficulties at the individual level:

   b. Possible difficulties at the family level:

   c. Possible difficulties with your own culture:

   d. Possible difficulties with other cultures:

   e. Possible difficulties with the society at large:

ACTIVITY VIII-4
Summarizing the Issues of Human Services Helping in a Multicultural Society

Imagine that it is your responsibility to explain the importance of the issues and the challenges of professionally helping people of cultural differentness. Although you have plenty of time to prepare, you have only three minutes in which to present to a renowned panel of multicultural experts the critical issues of professional human services work in a multicultural society. What key points or messages would you want to stress? Make a brief outline of your presentation below. If possible, collaborate with two persons of a different cultural background. Create your own outline or use the suggested structure below.

1. Critical issues in a multicultural society.

2. Key points regarding self-awareness of one's own cultural background.

3. Key points regarding awareness of cultural heritages and identities different from your own.

4. Issues of how awareness of self and awareness of others are critical to developing knowledge and skill in cross-cultural relationships.

5. Summarization.

SUMMARY OF SECTION VIII
Multiculturalism as a Force and Influence in Human Relationships

Reflect on the information developed in Section VIII. Try to identify the most critical ideas relevant to:

1. Your self-identity:

2. Your cross-cultural relationships:

3. Expanding your contacts with different others:

4. Suggestions for increasing your multicultural knowledge:

5. List any ideas you should be critically cautious about:

6. Based on your work in Section VIII, what message, idea, perception about multiculturalism would you like to share with yourself or your colleagues at this time?

7. As in previous sections, identify additional multicultural resources you have discovered during completion of Section VIII. We would further suggest that you now collate all the "source" charts of Sections I through VIII summaries. This single, larger document can be continuously expanded as you continue to develop your bases of multicultural awareness and knowledge.

SOURCE (book, film, etc.)	NATURE/TYPE OF SOURCE	WHERE TO FIND IT (address, phone, etc.)
1.		
2.		
3.		
4.		
5.		
6.		
7.		
8.		

IX

Selected Issues and Concerns in Multiculturalism

Background Reading: Chapters 1 through 11 in John A. Axelson, *Counseling and Development in a Multicultural Society* (3rd ed.). Pacific Grove, Calif.: Brooks/Cole, 1999.

In previous editions of this manual, an invitation was extended to the readers to contribute ideas and concerns relevant to their study of multicultural issues. This section presents several of those concerns as shared with the authors. Some arrived on scraps of paper, some were left on voice mail, and some were sent by instructors on behalf of an entire class. Most arrived anonymously and often did not identify supporting data relative to the issue shared. Other issues were identified in conversation with researchers, scholars, and professional human services practitioners in the field.*

Regardless of supportive data, we selected those concerns that seemed to be frequently raised and/or considered of unique importance. Our apologies for any particular inaccuracies in the presentation. As these are issues that readers took the time and energy to articulate, we consider them quite worthy of inclusion in this section. We hope to include more in future editions along with citing those who have shared their concerns with us. To this end we encourage all readers to complete Activity IX-3 and send the results to us.

We hope you will find the issues addressed to be meaningful to you. They have been to the authors and have prompted us to develop this section of the manual. We hope to continue and expand this effort in the future.

ACTIVITY IX-1
Concerns in Multiculturalism

A. Multiculturalism as a movement and a field of study is in the early stages of development. While the issues of cultural relationships are part of the history of the human race, the current widespread concern, diversity, and actions within the field

*In particular the authors appreciate the work of Professor Roger Herring, Ed.D., Dept. of Educational Leadership, University of Arkansas, Little Rock. Dr. Herring is one of the foremost scholars and researchers in the area of bi-racial and bi-ethnic relationships.

suggest it and its contents are perceived in widely differing manners by both those within as well as those "outside" the field. The terminology and language of its concepts, theory, and research are still undergoing the search to identify universally accepted definitions and terms to describe the human experience and condition. For example, terms such *as cross-cultural, transcultural, multicultural, bi-cultural, bi-ethnic, bi-racial, inter-cultural,* and *intra-cultural* have found their way into the literature. Any 10 persons may have 10 different meanings and definitions for each of these terms. And these are not just terms as in "words," but they often connote ideological, spiritual, and sociological postures of the user. Nevertheless, we often depend upon an expectation that others share the same understandings and meanings of words and events that we have. What difficulties must be confronted when this is not the case? What are the best strategies to implement when we are aware of differences in understandings?

B. Clarity of focus is also an issue when identifying what and who are considered most relevant to the content of this subject. Issues of "inclusion" versus "exclusion," cultural relations, race relations, internationalism/"one-worldism," oppression, a host of "-isms"—such as sexism, ageism, racism, anti-semitism—homophobia, and egaliatarianism abound. Is the focus to be upon "have" and/or "have-nots," majority and/or nonmajority (minority) persons? Are the distribution of wealth and power, political equality, human rights, forms of governance, and national/international economic systems of equal import? Even the concept of race and its meaning have become a large question—is it a valid and useful construct in today's world or an artificial construct inappropriately used to discriminate between populations of the world? What happens in a multicultural society such as the United States if a "blending" of heritages becomes the status quo of the citizenship?

C. Multiculturalism might still be described as a "new and emerging field." As such, the above issues and many more are part of the evolution of this movement and the development of an academic "-ology." In such an evolutionary process one of the most critical questions is what role participants will play in this movement. Who are to be considered the primary participants—that is, who are characterized as conductors ("shakers and movers") of ideas and actions? Who are the reactors ("on the receiving end") of such ideas? In particular, among helping professionals in the human services, is the focus to be upon "addressing needs" (as defined by whom?) and encouraging adjustment to what is? Or should the helper be actively advocating for change in societal institutions, processes, standards, and norms that may delimit opportunities for growth and development in the most healthful manner? For the professional perhaps the issue is one of clarifying who the client is—the individual client, the community, or perhaps both.

D. The content of multiculturalism may at times be simultaneously disheartening, confusing, vexing, creative, comforting, and uplifting. In essence it is volatile in nature. In purely intellectual discussions it might be addressed in a somewhat abstracted and nonemotional manner. However, in our daily lives it is often experienced in a most personal and intimate manner, generating any number and variety of emotions and behaviors. For example, some might find themselves, as they speak in a "politically correct" manner, also feeling that they cannot interact truthfully with another. In other words, presenting all concerns and thoughts, some of which might offend another (even with no intention of offending that person), is quite a challenge. Such experiences may make us overly cautious and reticent to share the very perceptions and feelings that may be most meaningful to improving a relationship with another who is "different" from ourselves. We run the risk of polarizing a relationship or of forming a relationship that might at best be shallow or at worst completely mislead another. Ultimately, each of us, in an effort to create meaningful relationships will face the challenge of being truthful and risking the difficulties that may ensue. Closely held beliefs and values may be threatened, and our sense of identity may be questioned; even our self-perceptions may be challenged at such times.

Some Questions to Consider

1. Does the concept of multiculturalism, in and of itself, present any difficulty for you? For others? Please explain.

2. What is your definition of the term *multiculturalism?* Does your definition state or imply that there should be a particular focus or social concern?

3. Given your definition of the term *multiculturalism,* are you aware of any difficulties others might have in accepting your definition as "the" definition?

4. Do you have a particular idea or intervention strategy that you think might have a powerful influence on improving relationships between people? What do others think of your idea?

5. Have you ever expected another to "know" what you mean, only to discover he or she did not at all? Or, did another person clearly understand the words spoken but misread your intent? Did this situation escalate in nonproductive ways?

6. How were you able to de-escalate the above situation and do you think some level of comfort (for each of you toward the other) was achieved?

7. What was learned from this experience that influences the way you now approach similar situations?

ACTIVITY IX-2
Issues in Multiculturalism

FOR YOUR CONSIDERATION

Statistics reported in U.S. Bureau of the Census documents as well as research literature and newspapers are ultimately based on the self-reports of respondents. As such, they may not be exact in fact; nevertheless, they may provide a measure of the racial/ethnic "blending" that has occurred in this society. Some of these numbers are provided here for your consideration. In 1993 the Bureau of the Census reported that 1 of every 20 marriages was reported as bi-racial. Census data of 1991 indicated there were over 1 million marriages between Euro-Americans and non–Euro-Americans. Approximately 20–25% of these were between Black Americans and Euro-Americans. Over 1 million marriages between Hispanic Americans and non-Hispanic-Americans were reported. It has been estimated that over 40% of Japanese American females married non-Japanese American males, and over 50% of Native American females married non-Native American males. Estimates of AmerAsian children residing in the United States equal 150,000 (generally thought to be a low figure), and that estimates of bi-ethnic youth in the United States range as high as 10 million.

A. Interracial Dating, Marriage, and Coupling

While dating and marriage between persons of different cultural heritage who are similar in the physical characteristics of ethnicity (for example, Irish and German) remain an issue of concern for some, such concern has diminished greatly in the United States. And while the difficulties of such interethnic couples within all culture groupings (in the past as well as the present) are by no means minimal, the interracial couple generally heightens concerns relative to cultural and racial group identity, cohesiveness, and continuity (of the group). In the United States as well as around the world, many members of any particular grouping often fear the disappearance not only of blood lines but also of long-held beliefs, values, and traditions when members begin to date, couple, or marry "outside" the group.

1. Are you, or someone you know, engaged in an interracial relationship? How many of such relationships are you personally aware of (among family and friends)?

2. How would you characterize the reactions to this (these) relationship(s)

   - by family?

   - by friends?

   - by others of your cultural background?

   - by people in general?

   - by specific organizations or institutions within the society?

3. What are the specific advantages or disadvantages of this relationship to the couple?

4. What are the specific advantages or disadvantages of this relationship to others?

5. What are the specific advantages or disadvantages of this relationship to the society?

B. Bi-racial Identity

"My father is Black and my mother is White. I always feel torn between them; that is, who am I to identify with? This usually happens depending on who I'm with. I get it from both sides! It sucks! Sometimes I just don't know what I'm supposed to do. Sometimes I even feel like I don't even know who I am. And one time I even blamed my parents for doing this to me instead of confronting those others."

Such statements and experiences are not uncommon among bi-racial youth and adults. While apparent racial differences between self and others usually present issues to be resolved, such differences between one's own parents presents another level of issue for the bi-racial person in most of their human relationships. Being classified by others as "belonging" to a particular cultural or racial grouping may be experienced as being forced to deny half of one's heritage. As one bi-racial person said, "I wouldn't let my mom 'out of the closet' for a long, long, time; especially during high school." (As an aside, bi-religiousity of parents may present similar issues; however, as these are not generally so obvious to others, they may be nonissues in many relationships and activities. For example, in parent-teacher conferences in a public school setting, the issue of religion would not generally be of large concern to the school, although the same might not be true within a parochial school system.) Of course when the "different race" parent or both show up for a conference, this cannot be "hidden" from teachers, other parents, and classmates and may alter the nature of many of the child's experiences.

1. Are you, or someone you know, a bi-racial person? How many bi-racial people do you know?

2. How would you characterize the reactions to this (these) person(s)

   • by your family?

   • by your other friends?

   • by others of your cultural background in general?

   • by others of the person's mother's racial/cultural background?

   • by others of the person's father's racial/cultural background?

   • by people in general (once they know)?

   • by specific organizations or institutions within the society?

3. Have you ever felt pressured to end your relationship or distance yourself from a friend who is bi-racial

- by family?

- by friends?

- by your friend's peers or your peers?

- by people in general?

4. Are you aware of any particular difficulties bi-racial persons experience that are clearly related to their bi-raciality? What has been your reaction to these difficulties in terms of your

- feelings?

- thoughts?

- behavior?

5. What might be some specific advantages or disadvantages of bi-raciality to

- the individual?

- the society?

C. Transcultural/Transracial/Transnational Adoption

FOR YOUR CONSIDERATION

In the late 1800s a train known as the "orphans' train" wended its way among major cities of the East (New York, Baltimore, etc.). It gathered and carried an estimated 100,000 orphans to be "given" to families throughout the Midwest and West who offered to provide homes for them. Today adoption agencies such as Welcome House (Doylestown, Pennsylvania) have brought many children from around the world to adoptive homes in the United States. State departments of children and family services also assist large numbers of youth and adults in both foster-care and adoption processes.

To some degree we all address the question of "Who am I"? We most often "discover" our answers to this self-identity question by the mere fact of living with our parents and family, neighbors and cultural heritage grouping as well as the society at large. However, for many adoptees both the question and many of the answers are not so clear or satisfying; that is, they don't get an answer to the question "once and for all." Looking for an answer to this question is often discomforting not only to the adoptee but also to those who nurtured the adoptee as well. Highly emotional issues , such as one's sense of identity, of belonging, of self-esteem, family loyalty, and even "worthiness for love" between parent and child are often raised. The movie *Secrets and Lies* speaks to many of these issues and is not at all unrelated to the experience of many adopted persons as they search for birth parents in an effort to discover answers that may be necessary to providing an answer to "Who am I?" Some questions address the reasons the child was given up; they may have queries as to how their birth parents have lived their lives; some are moving toward establishing relationships with siblings if there are any.

Each adoption situation is unique and raises some questions not so easily answered as they might be in the experience of children raised by their biological parents. However, differentness in racial heritage usually presents an array of additional issues for both child and parent. Physical differences characterized as race-related cannot be hidden within the family, let alone the community. "Simple" questions like "Who's your father?" or introducing your parents (who look different from you) may become quite emotionally painful to all—the child, the adoptive parents, and even the person asking the question.

In society at large there are organizations that will assist adoptees to find their birth parents. However, there are also laws pertaining to one's "right to know," which may conflict with other laws guaranteeing one's "right to privacy." The policies and procedures of any agency may also impede as well as assist in bringing birth parents (usually the mother) into contact with their adopted children. There are also associations and organizations that advocate for the adoption process to be permitted to occur only between adopting parents and children that share the same heritage. What once was generally perceived as simply "good people trying to do a good thing" has become a much larger issue today. For example, to what lengths should adoptive parents go in attempting to provide information about the child's heritage and race? In an age where couples might pay a woman to have a child for them, how much should be revealed? Is a birth parent who gave up her child but who has become "well off" over the years to be held responsible for that child's college expenses? Increasingly such issues have found their way into the courts.

1. Do you know anyone who is adopted? Do you know anyone who is adopted and is of a different racial heritage than his or her adoptive parents?

2. Are you aware of any particular concerns or difficulties experienced by either the adoptee or the adopting parents?

3. Do you think adoption should occur only between adults and children who share a particular ethnicity or race?

4. What legal, ethical, or social responsibilities toward a child do you think birth parents should be held accountable for in the case of adoption?

D. Classism

For Your Consideration

Robert B. Reich, a former president's cabinet member, wrote a book titled *Locked in the Cabinet* (Knopf, 1997; Vintage, 1998). The problems, paradoxes, and sometimes conflicts of loyalty while serving at that level of government but on behalf of the people of the United States are explored. Several issues related to the concept of classism in the United States and how a president and government are to respond are addressed. For example: How should such information be handled, and to whom should it be disseminated? What would be the repercussions throughout the society?

"The rich get richer, and the poor get poorer" is an old adage that continues to be of concern in the United States today. Reich's information suggests that the wealth of the United States has "grown" by one-third since 1985; it is also estimated that this new wealth is distributed among only the top 5–10% of the population. It is also estimated that over 40 million U.S. citizens have no medical insurance. Though salaries have increased over the past 15 years, they have not kept pace with the rate of inflation. Thus money today is worth less than the same amount yesterday.

Many parents in the middle socioeconomic group are wondering if their children will experience an increase or a decline in the standard of living they were able to achieve.

1. If you are a young person "starting out," do you expect to earn as much money as your parents have?

2. What are your parents' thoughts about this, and how do they think they could help you maintain at least an equivalent standard of living?

3. What particular impediments do you or your parents perceive to be the major obstacles you must overcome in order to achieve "the good life"?

4. What particular social or societal issues do you think place a great drain or strain on your efforts to do as well as, or better than, your parents?

Activity IX-3
Contributing to Multiculturalism in Today's World

Throughout this manual for learning, you have examined many issues, problems, and paradoxes of growing and developing in a multicultural society. Some of the material and questions have undoubtedly been vexing as well as demanding of your time. You are commended for the journey you have taken to explore, access, and develop your knowledge. Such awareness and knowledge as discovered and developed should provide you with an expanded framework for choosing the skills necessary for professional helping and personal living in this diverse nation.

Each of us in our ways of coming to know ourselves and the world around us becomes an expert in solving many of life's concerns and challenges. The authors hope that they have in some measure assisted you in developing greater expertise for life and living in this society. The authors would appreciate your input to their own growth and development as well as advice for improving this manual. We would be pleased to hear from you and would appreciate your responses to the questions that follow. We would appreciate it if you would identify yourself and provide a return address on any correspondence. Please forward your responses to:

Dr. John Axelson and Dr. Patrick McGrath
c/o Brooks/Cole Publishing Company
511 Forest Lodge Road
Pacific Grove, CA 93950-5098

Or send your ideas directly to:

Dr. Patrick McGrath
Dept. of Human Services
National-Louis University
Evanston, Illinois 60201

Questions

1. Is there any issue that you think we should address in future editions of this manual? Please articulate any aspects of the issue or idea that will help us more fully understand your concern.

2. Are you aware of or can you identify or create any idea or learning activity or make a suggestion that can be used to advance the knowledge base in multiculturalism and multicultural counseling and human services work?

3. What is your assessment of the usefulness of this manual and the background readings in improving your:

   a. Level of self-awareness?

   b. Level of awareness of others?

   c. Level of new multicultural knowledge and abilities further developed or prompted by use of this manual?

   d. Level of increased comfort in articulating and developing cross-cultural as well as same-cultural relationships?

4. Is there any content or activity that you believe needs to be clarified or improved upon?

   Name of content/activity:

   Page number:

   Suggestion for improvement:

5. Are there any other ideas about living in a multicultural society that you would like to share with the authors?

We thank you for your willingness to share your ideas and discoveries with us.

Patrick McGrath
John A. Axelson

A

Selected Resources for Diverse Populations

The books, agencies, associations, ethnic museums, movies, and theater plays listed on the following pages indicate the diversity of people, issues, and concerns within a multicultural society. In addition each community usually has a variety of agencies and associations that may be used as resources to develop and expand our cultural awareness of self and others. You are encouraged to explore your local community and develop a similar listing of culturally focused resources. Please recognize that the listings identify only a sample of the rich nature and array of resources addressing human diversity.

Movies and plays provide rich dramatizations of a variety of obvious as well as not-so-obvious issues and problems of life and living. They often present cultural and societal dilemmas and paradoxes that people have confronted in different eras as they resolve unique individual and family issues over the life span. Some, such as *Miss Saigon, Do the Right Thing*, and *The Power of One* address relationship difficulties and value/belief differences between individuals and groups of different cultural heritages. Others, such as *Jelly's Last Jam, The Crying Game, Like Water for Chocolate*, and *On Golden Pond*, present struggles people may have as they attempt to live in accord with the norms and expectations of their own family and cultural heritage. The following plays and movies are only a sample of what is available for our education and enjoyment.

Plays

American Buffalo by David Mamet
American Hurrah by Jean Claude van Itallie
Angels in America by Tony Keshner
Bent by M. Sherman
Boesman and Lena by Athol Fugard
Boys in the Band, The, by Mark Crowley
Cat on a Hot Tin Roof by Tennessee Williams

Chorus Line, A, by M. Bennet, M. Hamlisch, and others
Driving Miss Daisy by Alfred Uhry
Elephant Man, The, by Bernard Pomerance
Falsettoland by W. Finn and J. Lapine
For Colored Girls Who Have Considered Suicide When the Rainbow Is Enuf by Ntzoake Shange

Great White Hope, The, by Howard Sackler

Hair by G. Ragni and J. Rado

Heidi Chronicles, The, by Wendy Wasserstein

Hostage, The, by Brendan Behan

I'm Not Rappaport by Herb Gardner

Indians by Arthur Kopit

Jelly's Last Jam by George C. Wolf

Joe Turner's Come and Gone by August Wilson

Killing of Sister George, The, by Frank Marcus

Cage aux Folles, La, by H. Ferstein and J. Herman

M. Butterfly by David Henry Hwang

Ma Rainey's Black Bottom by August Wilson

Mass Appeal by Bill C. Davis

Master Harold and the Boys by Athol Fugard

Miss Saigon by Alain Boublil and Claude Michael Schonberg

Mother Courage and Her Children by Bertolt Brecht

Night of the Iguana, The, by Tennessee Williams

No Place to Be Somebody by Charles Gordone

Pacific Overtures by J. Weidman

Piano Lesson, The, by August Wilson

River Niger, The, by Joseph A. Walker

Royal Hunt of the Sun, The, by Peter Shaffer

Six Degrees of Separation by John Guare

Soldier's Play, A, by Charles Fuller

Staircase by Charles Dyer

Streamers by D. Rabe

Streetcar Named Desire, A, by Tennessee Williams

Suddenly Last Summer by Tennessee Williams

Taste of Honey, A, by Shelagh Delaney

Tiny Alice by Edward Albee

Toilet, The, by LeRoi Jones

Torch Song Trilogy by Harvey Feinstein

Who's Afraid of Virginia Woolf by Edward Albee

Movies/Videos

Many films, both past and current, are available in videotape format at local video rental outlet stores.

All Quiet on the Western Front
America, America
Amistad
And the Band Played On
Annie Hall
Avalon
Battle of Neretvam, The (Bitka na Neretvi)
Big Chill, The
Big Night
Birdcage, The
Birdman of Alcatraz
Blackboard Jungle, The
Black Robe
Born Yesterday
Bostonians, The
Boys in the Band, The
Boyz 'n the Hood

Braveheart
Breaking Away
Bridge on the River Kwai, The
Bridges at Toko-Ri, The
Bridges of Madison County, The
Broken Arrow
Bugsy
Carmen Jones
Caught in the Crossfire
Children's Hour, The
China Cry: A True Story
Chosen, The
Circle of Friends
City Lights
City of Hope
Clara's Heart
Claudine

Clockwork Orange, A
Color of Money, The
Color Purple, The
Conformist, The (Il Conformista)
Crimson Tide
Cry Freedom
Crying Game, The
Dances with Wolves
Dangerous Minds
Dead End
Deer Hunter, The
Desert Hearts
Diary of Anne Frank, The
Dim Sum: A Little Bit of Heart
Do the Right Thing
Dr. Zhivago
Driving Miss Daisy
Dry White Season, A
Educating Rita
Elephant Man, The
El Norte
Emerald Forest, The
Europa Europa (Hitlerjunge Salomon)
Evita
Exorcist, The
Family, The
Far and Away
Fiddler on the Roof
Field, The
Fried Green Tomatoes
Full Metal Jacket
Gandhi
Garden of the Finzi Continis, The
*   (Il Giardino dei Finzi-Contini)*
Gentleman's Agreement
G.I. Jane
Glory
Godfather, The, (Parts I, II, III)
Goodbye, Columbus
GoodFellas
Good Will Hunting
Grand Canyon
Grapes of Wrath, The
Great Santini, The
Guess Who's Coming to Dinner
Gunfight at O.K. Corral
Hair
Higher Learning
Hiroshima, Mon Amour

Hoop Dreams
House of Games, The
I Am a Fugitive from a Chain Gang
In Cold Blood
Indochina
In the Heat of the Night
Island in the Sun
Joy Luck Club, The
Jungle Fever
Just Another Girl on the I.R.T.
Killing Fields, The
Killing of Sister George, The
La Bamba
Lacombe Lucien
La Dolce Vita
Last Emperor, The
Last of the Mohicans, The
Last Wave, The
Lawrence of Arabia
Like Water for Chocolate
Little Big Man
Loneliness of the Long Distance
*   Runner, The*
Longest Day, The
Long Walk Home, The
Looking for Langston
Lord Jim
Lover, The
L-Shaped Room, The
Made in America
Make Way for Tomorrow
Making Love
Malcolm X
Marathon Man
Marjorie Morningstar
Marrying Kind, The
Mask, The
Medicine Man
Midnight Cowboy
Mi Familia
Mishima
Miss Evers' Boys
Mission, The
Mississippi Burning
Mississippi Masala
Mi Vida Loca
Moby Dick
Moonstruck
Mr. & Mrs. Loving

Mr. Deeds Goes to Town
Mr. Smith Goes to Washington
Murmur of the Heart (Le Souffle au Coeur)
Mutiny on the Bounty
My Beautiful Laundrette
My Man Godfrey
New Jack City
Nicholas and Alexandra
1900 (1976)
North to Alaska
Nun's Story, The
Of Mice and Men
Old Gringo
Once Upon a Time in America
Once Upon a Time in the West
*Once Upon a Time . . . When We Were
    Colored*
On Golden Pond
Ordinary People
Out of Africa
Passage to India, A
Passenger, The
Passion Fish
Pawnbroker, The
Piano, The
Platoon
Pocahontas
Power of One, The
Pretty Baby
Prizzi's Honor
Quigley Down Under
Raisin in the Sun, A
Rashomon
Red Corner
Reflections in a Golden Eye
Rich and Famous
River, The
Roots
Rose Tattoo, The
Rosewood
Running on Empty
Ryan's Daughter
Sarafina!
Saturday Night and Sunday Morning
Sayonara

Scarface
Schindler's List
School Daze
School Ties
Secrets and Lies
Separate but Equal
Sheltering Sky, The
She's Gotta Have It
Shoah
Shoot the Moon
Shy People
Silence of the Lambs, The
Slingblade
Sophie's Choice
Soul Food
Spook Who Sat by the Door, The
Staircase
Stand and Deliver
Stand by Me
Straight Out of Brooklyn
Taste of Honey, A
Taxi Driver
They Shoot Horses, Don't They?
This Boy's Life
Time to Kill, A
To Kill a Mockingbird
To Sir with Love
To Sleep with Anger
Two Left Feet
2001: A Space Odyssey
Unforgiven, The
Walk in the Clouds, A
Wedding, The
West Side Story
What's Eating Gilbert Grape
White Mischief
Witches of Eastwick, The
Witness
Woman of the Year
Women, The
Women of Brewster Place, The
World Apart, A
Year of Living Dangerously, The
Yentl
Zulu

Ethnic Museums

Ethnic museums are rich sources of cultural information that is often both historically and currently relevant. They also provide valuable information about members of other cultures, which may lead to greater appreciation of cross-cultural differences. The following list includes examples of some ethnic museums in the United States.

If you are interested in working on the internet to find out about ethnic museums, this URL is helpful: http://www.icom.org/vlmp/

African American Museum
Cleveland, OH
216-791-1700

The Balzekas Museum of Lithuanian
Culture and the Lithuanian Folk Art
Institute
Chicago, IL
773-582-6500

Chinese Culture Center
San Francisco, CA
415-986-1822

DuSable Museum of African American
History
Chicago, IL
773-947-0600

Harvard Semitic Museum
Cambridge, MA
617-495-4631

The Heard Museum
Phoenix, AZ
602-252-8840

Irish American Heritage Center
Chicago, IL
773-282-7035

Italian Cultural Center
Chicago, IL
708-345-3842

Japan Center
San Francisco, CA
415-557-4266

Mexican Fine Arts Center Museum
Chicago, IL
312-738-1503

Museum of Afro American History
Boston, MA
617-742-1854

Mitchell Indian Museum
Evanston, IL
847-475-1030

Oriental Institute Museum
Chicago, IL
773-702-9520

Peabody Museum of Archaeology
and Ethnology
Cambridge, MA
617-495-2248

Polish Museum of America
Chicago, IL
773-384-3352

Rosicrucian Egyptian Museum
San Jose, CA
408-947-3636

San Francisco African American
Historical/Cultural Society
San Francisco, CA
415-441-0640

Spertus Institute
Chicago, IL
312-922-9012

Swedish American Museum
Chicago, IL
773-728-8111

Ukrainian National Museum
Chicago, IL
773-276-6565

Museum of Tolerance
Los Angeles, CA
310-553-8403

Agencies and Associations

Many agencies, organizations, and associations are formed to address the needs of specific ethnic or racial cultural groups. Such agencies not only provide support to people as needed but also encourage pride in one's own heritage. They are also great sources of information about culturally different people. The following listings are examples of some agencies and associations in the United States. The letters in the parentheses indicate the state in which they are located.

If you are interested in finding many more agencies and associations, check a library for this reference book: *Encyclopedia of Associations,* 33rd edition, 1998, Gale Research, Detroit, MI.

African

American Committee on Africa,
    (212) 962-1210 (NY)
Ethiopian Community Development
    Council, (703) 685-0510 (VA)
Ghana Embassy, (202) 686-4520 (DC)
Operation Crossroads Africa,
    (212) 870-2106 (NY)
Organization of Nigerian Citizens,
    (410) 637-5165 (MD)

African American

African-American Cultural Alliance,
    (615) 299-0412 (TN)
African American Museums Association,
    (513) 376-4611 (OH)
Black Agenda, The, (614) 338-8383
    (OH)
Center for Multicultural Leadership
    (913) 864-3990 (KS)
National Association of African-
    American Chamber of Commerce,
    (214) 871-3060 (TX)
National Black Alcoholism Council,
    (202) 296-2696 (DC)

Asian

Asia Foundation, The, (415) 982-4640
    (CA) and (202) 588-9420 (DC)
Committee Against Anti-Asian Vio-
    lence, (212) 473-6485 (NY)
United States-Asia Institute,
    (202) 544-3181 (DC)

Bosnian

Bosnia Network, The, (205) 933-2159
    (AL)
Embassy of Bosnia and Herzegovina,
    (202) 833-3612 (DC)
Friends of Bosnia, (413) 586-6450 (MA)

Chinese American

Asian Human Services, (773) 728-2235
    (IL)
Chinese American Citizens Alliance,
    (213) 628-8015 (CA)
Chinese American Civic Council,
    (312) 225-0234 (IL)
Chinese Historical Society of America,
    (415) 391-1188 (CA)

Institute of Chinese Culture,
(212) 787-6969 (NY)
Organization of Chinese Americans,
(202) 223-5500 (DC)

Croatian

Consulate General of the Republic of
Croatia, (212) 599-3066 (NY)
Croatian Fraternal Union of America,
(412) 351-3909 (PA)
Embassy of Croatia, (202) 588-5899
(DC)

Gay and Lesbian

Archdiocesan Gay and Lesbian Out-
reach Chicago, (773) 525-3872 (IL)
Hetrick-Martin Institute, (212) 674-2400
(NY)
Horizons Community Service,
(773) 472-6469 (IL)
National Gay and Lesbian Task Force,
(202) 332-6483 (DC)
Parents, Families, and Friends of Lesbi-
ans and Gays, (202) 638-4200 (DC)
Pride Institute, (800) 54-PRIDE (CA)
Trikone, (408) 270-8776 (CA)

German American
(Anglo-Saxon)

American Historical Society of Germans
from Russia, (402) 474-3363 (NE)
German-American National Congress,
Inc., (773) 561-9181 (IL)
German Society of Pennsylvania, (215)
627-2332 (PA)

Haitian

Embassy of the Republic of Haiti,
(202) 332-4090 (DC)
Haitian Development Network,
(202) 661-4710 (DC), (212) 351-
5002 (NY), (801) 535-4358 (UT)
National Coalition of Haitian Rights,
(212) 337-0005 (NY)

Hispanic American

Foundation for the Advancement of
Hispanic Americans, (703) 866-1578
(VA)
Hispanic Housing Development Corpo-
ration, (312) 443-1260 (IL)
Institute for Latino Progress, Inc.,
(773) 890-0055 (IL)
League of United Latin American Citi-
zens, (915) 577-0726 (TX)
Latin American Chamber of Commerce,
(773) 252-5211 (IL)
Latino Institute, (312) 663-3603 (IL)
National Latino Communications
Center, (213) 663-8294 (CA)

Indian American (Asian)

Consulate General of India,
(415) 668-0683 (CA) and
(312) 595-0405 (IL)
Embassy of India, (202) 939-7000 (DC)
India Christian Association of America,
(708) 771-3177 (IL)
Indian Muslim Relief Committee,
(415) 856-0440 (CA)

Irish American

American Ireland Fund, (617) 574-0720
(MA)
Embassy of Ireland, (202) 462-3939
(DC)
Irish American Cultural Association,
(312) 238-7150 (IL)
Ireland Consulate General,
(312) 337-1868 (IL)
Irish Heritage Foundation,
(415) 621-2200 (CA)
Irish Institute, (718) 721-3363 (NY)

Italian American

American Italian Congress,
(718) 852-2929 (NY)
Italian-American Cultural Society,
(810) 751-2855 (MI)
United Italian American League,
(212) 486-6661 (NY)

Japanese American

Japanese American Citizens League,
    (415) 921-5225 (CA)
Japanese Foundation and Language
    Center, The, 310-449-0027 (CA)
Nippon Club, (212) 581-2223 (NY)
Urasenke Tea Ceremony Society,
    (212) 988-6161 (NY)

Jewish American

American Jewish Committee,
    (212) 751-4000 (NY)
Jewish Children's Bureau,
    (312) 444-2090 (IL)
Jewish Family and Children's Services,
    (602) 257-1904 (AZ)
Jewish Family Service, (714) 939-1111
    (CA)
Jewish Vocational Services,
    (312) 357-4500 (IL)

Mexican American

Mexican American Opportunity Foun-
    dation, (213) 890-9600 (CA)
Mexican American Unity,
    (210) 978-0500 (TX)

Native American

Americans for Indian Opportunity,
    (505) 867-0278 (NM)
American Indian Center, The,
    (773) 275-5871 (IL)
American Indian Health Service of
    Chicago, (773) 883-9100 (IL)
American Indian Heritage Foundation,
    (202) INDIANS (VA)
Gathering of Nations, (505) 836-2810
    (NM)
Indian Heritage Council,
    (423) 581-4448 (TN)
Maniilaq Association, (907) 442-3311
    (AK)
National American Indian Housing
    Council, (800) 284-9165 (DC)

Polish American

American Council for Polish Culture,
    (202) 414-9250 (DC)
Polish American Congress,
    (773) 763-9944 (IL)
Polish National Alliance,
    (773) 286-0500 (IL)
Polish Nobility Association Foundation,
    (410) 377-4352 (MD)
Polish Welfare Association,
    (773) 254-4444 (IL)

Puerto Rican

National Puerto Rico Forum,
    (212) 685-2311 (NY)
Puerto Rico Association for Community
    Affairs, (212) 673-7320 (NY)
Puerto Rican Family Institute,
    (212) 924-6320 (NY)

Russian

Congress of Russian Americans,
    (914) 358-7117 (NY)
Consulate General of the Russian
    Federation, (415) 202-9800 (CA)
Embassy of the Russian Federation,
    (202) 298-5700 (DC)

Tibetan

Tibet Fund, (212) 213-5011 (NY)
Tibetan Aid Project, (510) 848-4238
    (CA)

Vietnamese

Embassy of the Socialist Republic of
    Vietnam, (202) 861-0737 (DC)
Southeast Asia Resource Action Center,
    (202) 667-4690 (DC)
Vietnam Foundation, (703) 893-7458
    (VA)
Vietnam Refugee Aid, (703) 971-9178
    (VA)

Literature

Most community libraries are rich sourcees of cross-cultural information. Accessing both past and present writings about diverse people helps provide a framework for understanding human development in the context of family, culture, and societal events (and changes). The following list represents only a sample of writings pertinent to diverse populations.

African

Agbodeka, Francis, *Ghana in the 20th Century*
Asamoa, Ansa, *The Ewe of South-Eastern Ghana*
Hall, Edward, *Ghanaian Languages*

African American

Adams, Elizabeth, *Dark Symphony*
Allen, Chaney, *I'm Black and I'm Sober*
Angelou, M., *I Know Why the Caged Bird Sings*
Bates, Daisy, *The Long Shadow of Little Rock*
Baughman, Emmett Earl, *Black Americans*
Bibsby, C. W. E., *The Black American Writer, Vol. 1*
Browder, Tony, *The Browder Files*
Brown, Claude, *Manchild in the Promised Land*
Cartey, W., *Black Images*
Chapman, A. (Ed.), *Black Voices: An Anthology of Afro-American Literature*
Comer, James P., *Black Child Care*
Corrothers, James D., *In Spite of the Handicap*
Douglass, F., *My Bondage and Freedom*
Douglass, Frederick, *Narrative of the Life of Frederick Douglass, an American Slave*
DuBois, W. E. B., *Education of Black People, The*
DuBois, W. E. B., *Souls of Black Folk*
Evans, James, *Counseling the Black Client*
Farmer, J., *Lay Bare the Heart: An Autobiography of the Civil Rights Movement*
Gregory, Dick (with Robert Lipsyte), *Nigger*
Grier, W. H. and Cobbs, P. M., *Black Rage*
Griffin, J. H., *Black Like Me*
Hacker, George, *Marketing Booze to Blacks*
Harris, Eddy, *Mississippi Solo*
Harris, Eddy, *Native Stranger*
Harris, Eddy, *South of Haunted Dreams: A Ride Through Slavery's Old Back Yard*
Hazelden Foundation, *Alcohol and Drug Abuse in Black America*
Hazelden Foundation, *Black, Beautiful and Recovering*
Hazelden Foundation, *Counseling Ethnic Minorities*
Herndon, Angelo, *Let Me Live*
Hernton, C. C., *Sex and Racism in America*
Holtzclaw, William H., *The Black Man's Burden*
Huggins, Nathan, *Harlem Renaissance*
Joseph, S. M. (Ed.), *The Me Nobody Knows: Children's Voices from the Ghetto*

Liebow, E., *Tally's Corner: A Study of Black Streetcorner Men*
Malamud, B. *Idiots First*
Malcolm X (with assistance of Alex Haley), *The Autobiography of Malcolm X*
Memoirs of a Monticello Slave: The Life of Isaac Jefferson
Parks, Gordon, *A Choice of Weapons*
Redding, J. Saunders, *No Day of Triumph*
Russell, Bill (as told to William McSweeny), *Go Up for Glory*
Southern, E., *The Music of Black Americans*
Thomas, Will, *The Seeking*
Washington, Booker T., *Up from Slavery*
Waters, Ethel (with Charles Samuels), *His Eye Is on the Sparrow*
White, Walter, *A Man Called White*
Wiley, Ralph, *Why Black People Tend to Shout*
Wright, Richard, *Black Boy*

Anglo-Saxon American

Bernays, Susan, *Growing Up Rich*
Birmingham, Stephen, *Our Crowd*
Brookhiser, Richard, *The Way of the WASP: How It Made America and How It Can Save It . . . So to Speak*

Asian American (General)

Chin, F., Chan, J. P., Inada, L. F., and Wong, S. H. (Eds.), *Aiiieeeee! An Anthology of Asian-American Writers.*

Chinese American

Buck, Pearl S., *The Good Earth*
Chen, Pearl Kong, *Everything You Want to Know about Chinese Cooking*
Clayse, Alasdair, *The Heart of the Dragon*
Green, James W., *Cultural Awareness in the Human Services*
Kingston, Maxine Hong, *China Men*
Kingston, Maxine Hong, *Women Warriors*
Peck, Stacy, *Halls of Jade, Walls of Stone: Women in China Today*
Tan, Amy, *The Joy Luck Club*

German American

Deighton, Len, *Winter*
French, Irene M., *The German-American Heritage*
Hobbie, M., *An Annotated Directory of German Immigrant Culture in the U.S. and Canada*
Hofmeister, Rudolph A., *The Germans of Chicago*
Johann, Ernst, *German Cultural History of the Last Hundred Years*
Jones, G. F., *German-American Names*
O'Connor, Richard, *The German-Americans: An Informal History*
Peckinpah, Sam, *Cross of Iron*

Pochmann, H., *German Culture in America, Philosophical and Literary Influences*
Ripley, LaVern, *The German-Americans*
Ripley, LaVern, *German Traditions of German Ways*
Russ, Jennifer M., *German Festivals and Customs*
Sajer, Guy, *Forgotten Soldier*
Schweieder, E., *A Peculiar People, Iowa's Old Order Amish*

Hispanic American

Brogan, Nancy L., and Devine, Elizabeth, *Latin America, Social Life and Customs*
de Jesus, Carolina Maria, *Child of the Dark: The Diary of Carolina Maria de Jesus*
Galarza, E., *Barrio Boy*
Harth, D. E., and Baldwin, L. M. (Eds.), *Voices of Aztlan: Chicago Literature of Today*
Kiev, A., *Curanderismo: Mexican-American Folk Psychiatry*
Lewis, O., *The Children of Sanchez*
Lewis, O., *Five Families: Mexican Case Studies in the Culture of Poverty*
Manguel, Albert (Ed.), *Other Fires, Short Fiction by Latin American Women*
Padilla, Ellen, *Up from Puerto Rico*
Steinbeck, John, *Tortilla Flat*
Thomas, P., *Down these Mean Streets*
Valdez, L., and Steiner, S. (Eds.), *Aztlan: An Anthology of Mexican American Literature*
Weyr, Thomas, *Hispanic U.S.A., Breaking the Melting Pot*

Indian American (Asian)

Abrams, H. N., *India—Civilization, Festival of India in the United States*
Boyd, Doug, *India—Religion*
de Combray, Richard, *Caravansary*
Guellous, Ezzedine, *Mecca, The Muslim Pilgrimage*
McCellan, Grant S., *India: A Reference Shelf*
McDermott, Robert A., *India—Intellectual Life, The Spirit of Modern India: Writings in Philosophy, Religion and Culture*
Mehta, Ved, *The New India: A Searching; Compassionate Look at the World's Most Populous Democracy in the Light of Indira Ghandhi's Rise and Fall*
Mohanti, Prafulla, *My Village. My Life: Portrait of an Indian Village*
Naipaul, V. S., *India: A Wounded Civilization*
Spear, Pervical, *India: A Modern History*

Irish American

Birmingham, S., *Real Lace: America's Irish Rich*
Birmingham, Stephien, *Irish in the U.S*
Cleary, James, *Proud Are We Irish*
Eagleton, Terry, *Nationalism, Colonialism, and Literature*
Foster, R. F., *Modern Ireland, 1600–1972*
Harkness, David, *Northern Ireland since 1920*
Keough, Dermot, *The Rise of the Working Class*
Nolen, Janet, *Ourselves Alone: Women's Emigration from Ireland 1885–1920*
O'Brien, Edna, *Tales for the Telling: Irish Folk and Fairy Stories*

O'Faolain, Sean, *The Irish. A Character Study*
Shannon, William, *The American Irish*
Sotto Press, *O Come Ye Back to Ireland*

Italian American

Ardizzone, T., *The Evening News*
Ets, M. H., *Rosa: The Life of an Italian Immigrant*
Fast, H. M., *The Immigrants*
Fast, H. M., *Second Generation*

Japanese American

Kitagawa, D., *Issei and Nisei: The Internment Years*

Jewish American

Ben-Sasson, H. H., and Ett, Inger, *Jewish Society Through the Ages*
Berman, Rabbi Susan, *The Twelve Steps and Jewish Tradition*
Epstein, Perle, *Kabbalah, The Way of the Jewish Mystic*
Ouispel, G., *Jewish and Agnostic Man*
Reimer, J., *Jewish Reflections on Death*
Shoelson, Abraham B., *Marriage and Family: A Jewish View*
Twerski, Rabbi Abraham J., *Self-Discovery in Recovery*
Unterman, A., *Jews: Their Religious Beliefs and Practices*
Wiesel, Elie, *Night*
Wouk, Herman, *This Is My God*

Laotian American

Donver, Arthur J., *Laos: Keystone of Indo China*
Proudfoot, Robert, *Even the Birds Don't Sound the Same Here: The Laotian Refugees
    Search for Heart in American Culture*
Whitaker, Donald P., *Laos: A Country Study*

Native American

Allen, T. (Ed.), *The Whispering Wind: Poetry by Young American Indians*
Armstrong, V. I., *I Have Spoken: American History Through the Voices of Indians*
Benchley, Nathaniel, *Only Earth and Sky Last Forever*
Brant, Beth (Ed.), *A Gathering of Spirit: A Collection by North American Indian Women*
Brant, C. S., *Jim Whitewolf: The Life of a Kiowa Apache Indian*
Brown, D., *Bury My Heart at Wounded Knee*
Brown, D., *Creek Mary's Blood*
Deloria, V., *Custer Died for Your Sins: An Indian Manifesto*
Gunn Allen, Paula, *The Sacred Hoop: Recovering the Feminine in American Indian
    Traditions*
Lame Deer, John Fire, *The Life of Sioux Medicine Man*

Niehardt, John G., *Black Elk Speaks: Visions of an American Indian*
Pratson, J. F., *Land of the Four Directions: A Portrait of North American Indian Life Today*
Richter, C., *The Light in the Forest.*
Storm, Hyemeyohsts, *Seven Arrows.*
Uizener, Gerald, *Crossbloods: Bone Courts, Bingo and Other Reports.*
Waddell, J. O., and Watson, O. M. (Eds.), *The American Indian in Urban Society.*

Norwegian American

Rolvaag, O. E., *Giants in the Earth*

Polish American

Ascherson, Neal, *The Struggle for Poland*
Haiman, Miecislaus, *Poles in New York, 17th and 18th Century*
Michener, James A., *Poland*
Radlowski, Roger J., and Kirvan, John J., *The Spirit of Poland*
Schaufele, William E., *Polish Paradox*
Zieleniewicz, Andrezej, *Poland.*

Scottish American

Burns, Robert, *Poems*
Manley, Sean, *My Heart's in the Heather*

Swedish American

Judson, C. I., *They Came from Sweden*
Lorenzen, L., *Of Swedish Ways*

Vietnamese American

Matthews, E., *Culture Clash: A Vietnamese Family*

Gay and Lesbian

Bérubé, Allan, *Coming Out under Fire*
Boswell, John, *Christianity, Social Tolerance and Homosexuality*
Browning, Frank, *Culture of Desire*
Comstock, Gary David, *Gay Theology without Apology*
Driggs, J., and Finn, S., *Intimacy between Men*
Dubeman, M., et al., *Hidden from History*
Foucault, Michel, *The History of Sexuality*
Gerber, Marjorie, *Vested Interests*
Green, Michelle, *The Dream at the End of the World*
Hazelden Foundation, *Gay and Lesbian Alcoholics: AA's Message of Hope*
Hazelden Foundation, *Lesbian and Gay Issues in Early Recovery*
Money, John, *Gay, Straight and In-between*

Paglia, Camille, *Sexual Personae*
Parkside (Agency), *Worthy of Recovery*
Rist, Darell Yates, *Heartland*
Shilts, Randy, *Conduct Unbecoming*
Signoile, Michelangelo, *Queer in America*
Thompson, Mark, *Gay Spirit*
Tripp, C. A., *The Homosexual Matrix*

Men and Women

Adler, Leonore Loeb (Ed.), *Women in Cross-Cultural Perspective*
Bergmann, Barbara R., *The Economic Emergence of Women*
Bly, Robert, *Iron John*
Chesler, Phyllis, *Women and Madness.*
Gilligan, Carol, *In a Different Voice: Psychological Theory and Women's Development*
Gornick, Vivian, and Moran, Barbara K. (Eds.), *Women in Sexist Society: Studies in Power and Powerlessness*
Miller, Jean Baker, *Toward a New Psychology of Women*
Mitchell, Juliet, *Psychoanalysis and Feminism*
Ms. (magazine)
Reskin, Barbara F., and Roos, Patricia A., *Job Queues, Gender Queues: Explaining Women's Inroads into Male Occupations*
Robbins, Joan H., *Knowing Herself: Women Tell Their Stories in Psychotherapy*
Rotundo, E. Anthony, *American Manhood*
Working Mother (magazine)

B

Additional Questionnaire and Forms for Use in Interviewing Your and Other Cultural Groups

The questionnaire and forms that follow ought to help you further organize and examine the data you discovered in interviewing family members as well as people of different heritages and/or experiential background.

SELF-CULTURAL EXPLORATION PROJECT
(Family Member Interview)

The purpose of this assignment is to allow you to explore and examine your own background, identify prejudices and biases, perceptions and beliefs, and so on. Families are transmitters of cultural beliefs and values passed on from generation to generation. Interviewing your oldest family member may help you identify those beliefs and values that are more likely culture based rather than unique only to your family. The following questions, asked of yourself and/or the family member being interviewed, should assist you in developing self-awareness of your own cultural heritage.

1. What *is* your cultural heritage background? Is it mono-, bi-, or multicultural?

   a. What has it meant to belong to your culture group? (For example, do you feel you have more or less privileges as a member of your cultural group?)

   b. How has it felt to belong to your culture group?

   c. What do you like about your culture identity?

   d. What do you dislike?

2. If you have a bi- or multiheritage, do you "claim" all or primarily one?

   a. If one, why that one and not the other(s)?

   b. Is there more privilege, power, and so on with one versus the other?

   c. Did your family "skew" your heritage in one direction over the other?

3. a. Where did you grow up, and what other culture groups resided there?

   b. What was the quality of the relationship among these groups?

4. What are the values of the cultural heritage groups you *most* identify with?

5. What was your first experience of noticing you are "different" from others?

6. a. What are your earliest images of race, color, ethnicity?

   b. What information were you given about how to deal with such issues?

7. a. Identify all of the identity groups to which you belong (e.g., gender, ethnic, socioenonomic, sexual orientation, and so on).

   b. Rank order the groups from those that have the most influence on your identity to those that have the least influence. Explain your ranking.

8. Discuss your experiences as a person having or lacking power in relation to the following: ethnic identity; racial identity; within the family; class identity; sexual identity; and professional identity.

Adapted from Sue Brotherton, Ph.D., University of California, Santa Barbara, by Patrick McGrath, Ed.D.

9. a. What are your feelings toward the family member you interviewed?

   b. Do you have different or similar beliefs, values, perceptions, biases? Why might this be so?

10. Other thoughts/information?

11. Offer some concluding remarks.

CULTURE GROUP IN PROFILE, BY:

Primary descriptors:	*Secondary descriptors:*

List major characteristics of this group. Include information that addresses critical values, perceptions of the world, and/or the major historical experiences of the culture. Categorize this information as to whether it is similar/dissimilar to your own culture.

Similar	*Dissimilar*

List critical information relevant to understanding this culture:

List key ideas and behaviors that would increase the likelihood of being able to relate well to this culture:

Summary statement regarding this culture:

CULTURE HERITAGE GROUP IN PROFILE FORM

Name_____

The following information represents your understanding of your own cultural group according to your self-culture interview as well as perceptions based on knowledge achieved from any other source of information.

GROUP

Primary descriptors—national origins, physical and behavioral characteristics, and so on:

Secondary descriptors—list characteristics of this group. Include information that addresses:

Values/beliefs:

Perceptions of the world:

Methods of settling conflicts:

Methods of ensuring conformity:

Group personality:

Relationship to other groups:

Important to achieve (in lifetime):

Major historical events:

Other critical information relevant to understanding this culture:

1.

2.

3.

4.

5.

6.

7.

List key ideas and behaviors that would increase the likelihood of being able to relate well to this culture:

Summary statement regarding this culture:

COMPARING CULTURAL INFORMATION FORM A—SIMILARITIES

Develop comparison charts of your culture and another you investigated identifying significant characteristics (i.e., similarities and differences to/from these cultures) utilizing information obtained in your interviews, readings, and so on.

Name_____

Culture Interviewed:	Culture of Self:

Significant myths/folklore/legends:

General traits (physical/biological, etc.):

Beliefs/values (religious/interpersonal/social):

View of the world (time, nature, and so on):

Personality of culture (behavioral orientation):

Specific cultural issues:

Achievement (what's important and how to "get it," life goals):

Family structure/organization (patterns/size/inclusion):

Methods of enforcing conformity (transmitting values/behavior):

Child-rearing practices (who's responsible/approaches):

Gender relationships

Male to male:

Female to female:

Female to male:

Male to female:

Societal realities (historical and current):

Other:

COMPARING CULTURAL INFORMATION FORM B—DISSIMILARITIES

Develop comparison charts of your culture and another you investigated identifying significant characteristics (i.e., similarities and differences to/from these cultures) utilizing information obtained in your interviews, readings, and so on.

Name_____

Culture Interviewed:	Culture of Self:

Significant myths/folklore/legends:

General traits (physical/biological, etc.):

Beliefs/values (religious/interpersonal/social):

View of the world (time, nature, and so on):

Personality of culture (behavioral orientation):

Specific cultural issues:

Achievement (what's important and how to "get it," life goals):

Family structure/organization (patterns/size/inclusion):

Methods of enforcing conformity (transmitting values/behavior):

Child-rearing practices (who's responsible/approaches):

Gender relationships

Male to male:

Female to female:

Female to male:

Male to female:

Societal realities (historical and current):

Other:

C

Journal of Critical Thoughts in Multiculturalism: A Record of Reactions to Multicultural Experiences

"Critical Thoughts" are observations, ideas, feelings, and even questions you may have about any of the readings, activities, and discussion in *Accessing Awareness and Developing Knowledge: Foundations for Skill in a Multicultural Society.* Other relevant thoughts may also be "discovered" as you go to work, do your shopping, go to the movies, read a book or newspaper, attend recreational events and so on. These thoughts are important to your understanding of the impact of culture on life and living. To further develop your awareness of such experiences and your thoughts and perceptions about those experiences, you are encouraged to share, compare, and discuss these with others—family, friends, classmates, instructors, coworkers.

While the following form is categorically structured, you are not required to record some thought in every category. There is also no required number of items. Record as many or as few as you choose form week to week. Reproduce this form so that you will have one copy for each week that you are working with this book. A summarization page for your thoughts is also provided.

Finally, please consider this journal, though serious, to be fun! Let your thoughts range as far afield as you want. Be as creative and theoretical as you wish.

CRITICAL THOUGHTS ON MULTICULTURAL EXPERIENCES	Week _____ Date _____
From assignments/duties for school, work, family, church, etc.:	
From discussions with family, friends, classmates, coworkers, etc.:	
From readings (novels, newspapers, magazines, etc.):	
From television programs, movies, and plays:	
Other:	

Summary of critical thoughts: The following ideas, are what I consider to be of most import in understanding the influence of cultural heritage on self and others.

Note: The numbers 1–13 do not indicate an expectation of 13 thoughts; record as many or as few as you choose!

1.

2.

3.

4.

5.

6.

7.

8.

9.

10.

11.

12.

13.

TO THE OWNER OF THIS BOOK:

We hope that you have found *Accessing Awareness and Developing Knowledge, Foundations for Skill in a Multicultural Society*, Third Edition, useful. So that this book can be improved in a future edition, would you take the time to complete this sheet and return it? Thank you.

School and address: _____

Department: _____

Instructor's name: _____

1. What I like most about this book is: _____

_____

_____

2. What I like least about this book is: _____

_____

_____

3. My general reaction to this book is: _____

_____

4. The name of the course in which I used this book is: _____

_____

5. Were all of the chapters of the book assigned for you to read? _____

   If not, which ones weren't? _____

6. In the space below, or on a separate sheet of paper, please write specific suggestions for improving this book and anything else you'd care to share about your experience in using the book.

_____

_____

_____

_____

_____

_____

_____

_____

_____